# YESTERDAY'S CHILDREN
## A Longitudinal Study of Children from Kindergarten into the Adult Years
By Philip E. Kraus
Foreword by Arthur T. Jersild

*Yesterday's Children* is one of the few longitudinal studies, and the most extensive, to focus on the child in a school and learning setting. It follows 165 children—black, white, Hispanic, and Oriental—from the day they entered kindergarten through the sixth grade. Approximately half of the children were followed through high school and information on more than a score was obtained at the adult level as well.

The book answers such questions as—
*How do black children progress in classrooms of black teachers as compared with white teachers?*
*What happens to children who experience continual failure in school?*
*How effectively do teachers identify giftedness and talents?*
*How early can we predict school performance?*
*How do severe traumatic home experiences affect school progress and behavior?*
*How do tests and testing affect children?*
*To what extent are teachers influenced by children's test scores?*
*How do the aspirations of white and black parents differ?*

Avoiding a statistical approach, the study treats the children in human terms as it covers topics including intelligence, reading achievement, the failures, the accelerated, the promise of giftedness, children with problems, fearful children, and other topics.

This unique study challenges many long-standing and widely held beliefs in the fields of education and psychology. It will be of great interest to psychologists, school administrators, guidance counselors, and teachers. Students in child development and in teacher-training programs will find material which will be of great significance in increasing their perception and understanding of the educational process.

Children

### e Author
. KRAUS is Professor of Edu-
Hunter College of the City
y of New York. Among his pre-
sitions, Dr. Kraus was Coor-
f the Hunter College Campus
Project Director in the New
Board of Education, a teacher
cipal in New York City schools,
sychiatric case worker and
gist in a child care agency. He
thor of *Diagnosis and Special*
*n in Reading* and of numerous
nal pamphlets and articles in
ional journals. Dr. Kraus
the Ph.D. degree in educa-
ychology at New York Univer-

# YESTERDAY'S CHILDREN

A Longitudinal Study of
Children from Kindergarten
into the Adult Years

**PHILIP E. KRAUS**

Hunter College
of the
City University of New York

**A Wiley-Interscience Publication**

JOHN WILEY & SONS,  New York · London · Sydney · Toronto

*Library of Congress Cataloging in Publication Data*

Kraus, Philip E        date
    Yesterday's children.

    "A Wiley-Interscience publication."
    Bibliography: p.
    1. Child study. I. Title.

BF721.K69        370.15        72–10125
ISBN 0–471–50722–9

Printed in the United States of America

10 9 8 7 6 5 4 3 2 1

To Our Children
and
Their Teachers

# Foreword

Longitudinal investigations, with follow-up studies of the same population during childhood years, or from childhood into adult life, represent the most important contributions to developmental psychology. Such illustrious investigators as Terman, Gesell, and Shirley are among the pioneers in this line of study.

The present longitudinal study by Dr. Philip E. Kraus offers a unique and important addition to this valuable literature.

The basic population consisted of 165 children—black, white, Hispanic, and Oriental—who participated in the study from the day they entered kindergarten until they had finished the sixth grade. The children originally attended two New York City schools, one in Brooklyn and one in Harlem. Most of them (148) remained to complete the ninth grade.

A large number of the children (85) were followed through the high school years, and information concerning more than a score of these was obtained also at the adult level. This is the most extensive longitudinal study that centers mainly on the child in a school setting. It deals with perennial questions and also, in a most timely manner, with current issues pertaining to the education of black and white children.

Dr. Kraus' data provide information on questions such as the following:

How do black children progress in classrooms of black teachers as compared with white teachers?

What becomes of those children who have serious difficulty when leaving their parents on entrance to school?

How effectively do teachers identify talents and giftedness?

Do children who present early behavior problems in school eventually "grow out of it"?

How do open classrooms and classroom structure affect children?

How do tests and testing affect children?

To what extent are teachers influenced by children's test scores?

How have children's self-concepts and ethnic awareness changed in the last two decades?

How early can we predict school performance?

How do the aspirations of white and black parents differ?

How do severe traumatic home experiences affect children's school progress and behavior?

What happens to children who experience continual failure in school and must repeat classes?

Although the study was able to follow closely only 165 children from middle and low socioeconomic areas, it actually had contact with more than 1000 children. Unlike some studies of its kind, it treats children not as statistics but in warm, human terms. The results challenge many long-standing and widely held beliefs in the fields of education and psychology.

This unique study should be of great interest to psychologists, school administrators, guidance counselors, teachers, and students in child development and in teacher-training programs.

ARTHUR T. JERSILD

*Professor Emeritus of*
  *Psychology and Education*
*Teachers College*
*Columbia University*

# Preface

The school experience, as a part of the life of an American child, has frequently been discussed in terms of school organization, educational practices, or teacher-pupil interaction. This longitudinal study describes it in relation to its impact on children and their reactions and performance over a period of two decades. The questions raised in Chapter One were the immediate goals of the project, but as work progressed new questions arose, and our experiences and observations provided answers to other unanticipated questions, and additional conclusions concerning children's growth and development through the elementary, junior, and senior high school years, and well beyond.

The research population entered the kindergartens of two schools in 1953. A small group of children of the same age were added to these in the first and second grades. Since the focus was on the school experience, parental cooperation, though desirable, was not a prerequisite for children's remaining in the study. Our children completed the sixth grade in 1960, the junior high school in 1962 or 1963, and at least half of their number was graduated from high school in 1966. Those who attended college received their degrees in 1970. Wherever possible, anecdotal material contains the verbatim comments of the children or of their teachers. This should convey to the reader the qualitative aspects of the situations described.

At the inception of this study there was no intent to distinguish between black and white children in their growth and development. However, the changing social climate of the last two decades and the increasing number of psychological and sociological studies of differences warranted a reexamination of the data. It should not be surprising that among black and white children of equal ability, the similarities in progress and in parental attitudes are greater than the differences. These are indicated in Chapter Nine.

For measures of achievement, we relied essentially on standardized tests given citywide. We devised our own scales and questionnaires to obtain teacher and parent judgments and reactions. These proved to be very productive in our assessment of children.

It is our hope that the findings and conclusions of this study will help those who seek a sober evaluation of current school programs and their impact upon children, and will serve as a guide to the identification and encouragement of promising practices in an urban setting.

PHILIP E. KRAUS

*November 1972*
*New York, New York*

# Acknowledgments

In a project that involved very many people, it is impossible to isolate the contributions of any one person. I am, however, grateful to all who gave their time and expertise to this study.

With one exception, members of the original Planning Committee were associate superintendents, assistant superintendents, or directors of bureaus in the New York City Board of Education. I hope I will be forgiven if I do not indicate titles in listing their names. They were William Bristow, Hannah Kostiner, Morris Krugman, May Lazar, Jean Thompson, Rebecca Winton, J. Wayne Wrightstone, and Charlotte Winsor of the Bank Street College of Education. Also of inestimable help on this committee were the late Florence Beaumont, Ethel Huggard, Jacob Shack, and Frances Wilson.

At various times in the early stages of the study, Mary Fitzgerald, Rose Goldman, Vivienne Hochman, Irma Mohr, Alma Paulsen, Theophilia Phillips, Martha G. Shapp, and Helen Winfield served as consultants.

From 1952 to 1963 the study was under the aegis of Dr. J. Wayne Wrightstone, Assistant Superintendent in charge of Educational Research. Working with him was a rich learning experience and I am deeply grateful for his guidance, his support, and his friendship. It was through his intervention and with his assistance that in 1963 I was able to take with me to Hunter College all the data and files of the study so that I could continue the research independently.

Merely listing the names of my former staff is hardly adequate recognition for their contributions. Many of the findings and conclusions are as much the result of their experiences and thinking as they are of mine. Gertrude P. Bonime was the original Project Assistant assigned to the Jefferson School. Her human relations skills laid the basis of our effectiveness there, and she subsequently resigned from the project to become the school's assistant principal. She was succeeded by Mildred Mendelson, who moved on with the Jefferson School children through the junior high school. From 1960 through 1963, when Board of Education support ended, she was the sole remaining staff member. However, her personal relationships with many of the children continued for many years. Ruth Liebers was the original Project Assistant at the Washington School, where she remained with the children from 1953 through 1960, when they completed the sixth grade. Miriam F. Lieberman also served as Project Assistant in the Washington School from 1955 to 1959, sharing with Ruth Liebers the large school population. Both were present when the school burned and recorded the drama described in Chapter Eight.

The case histories were written by Mildred Mendelson and Ruth Liebers. I trust I have done them no injustice by adding details and events beyond the elementary and junior high school years. In addition to their functions in their respective schools, each staff member assumed responsibilities consistent with her special skills. Ruth Liebers wrote the major part of one publication, *Skillful Teaching Practices in the Elementary Schools,* and parts of various interim reports; Mildred Mendelson assisted with the editing of all publications and interim reports, and organized systems for recording the data that were being gathered; Miriam F. Lieberman provided individual psychological testing for some children who could not be accommodated at local psychological clinics.

From 1953 to 1957 Marcella Draper, research assistant, and Judith Krugman, research psychologist, joined the staff one day each week to take part in the weekly conferences and, occasionally, in observations. Their contributions were out of all proportion to the time they spent with us. They were responsible for the publication *Report of Orientation Programs in Kindergarten and First Grade.*

I should like to thank the many teachers and principals who worked with our children and who cooperated with us with such enthusiasm. Never did we feel resentment when we sat in classrooms, nor impatience when we interrupted their schedules.

I am indebted to many others—to Arthur T. Jersild for his wise suggestions and encouragement, and to Herbert Schueler, former Director of Teacher Education at Hunter College, for providing clerical assistance during 1964. Beginning in 1966, small annual grants from the Tuch Foundation for clerical and secretarial assistance made possible the duplication and mailing of questionnaires, correspondence, and most important, the preparation of this manuscript. Without this help, the project could not have been completed.

Finally, I am deeply grateful to my own family. I want to thank my children, Lucy, Alice, and Robert, who at various times in their young lives found themselves answering questions and questionnaires, and unknowingly helping to refine first drafts of instruments we planned to use. I am most indebted to my wife, Martha, who shielded me from chores and interruptions and acted as a sounding board for my ideas. Her suggestions were invaluable and her editing of the manuscript improved it immeasurably. The countless other ways in which she assisted are known only to women whose husbands are writing.

P. E. K.

# Contents

# CHAPTER ONE

## Introduction

Each decade of the twentieth century has seen educational movements surge and subside, but no decade has shown the upheavals and turmoil of the 1960s. The Progressive Education movement of the 1920s and 1930s had its severe critics, whose cause was furthered by practitioners who misinterpreted Dewey's principles and philosophy. Nevertheless, the widespread dissatisfaction with public education and the search for solutions to difficult problems did not reach their energetic and somewhat frenetic stage until the 1960s and 1970s.

History may record the 1960s as the decade of educational innovations. Curricular development saw the emergence of courses in new mathematics and new physics. Adaptations in other areas in the rearrangement of course content moved college courses into the high school and high school subjects and topics into the junior high schools or elementary schools.

Innovations in school organization and in teaching techniques and processes were impressive. Closed-circuit television (CCTV), programmed instruction, language laboratories, and team teaching became new ways of conveying information and knowledge and of stimulating learning. More recently, performance contracting, industry's guarantee of pupil progress, became a new panacea. Many newly formed commercial organizations undertook this responsibility, claiming they had answers to the complex problems of learning that had eluded professional educators for many years.

These changes have been referred to as "the educational revolution." Measuring their impact upon children requires rigorous and objective evaluation. This has not always been possible, and attempts to evaluate specific programs have produced inconclusive results.

There are conflicting reports (Woodring, 1970) of the effectiveness of CCTV, language laboratories have not always proven their worth, and team teaching has solved more teaching problems than learning problems (Polos, 1965). Furthermore, new mathematics has not raised perceptibly the national level of children's achievements (Sarason, 1970), and in summarizing evaluations of performance contracting, the U. S. Office of Economic Opportunity states, "The results . . . clearly indicate that the firms operating under performance contracts did not perform significantly better than the more traditional school systems. Indeed, both control and experimental students did equally poorly in terms of achievement gains, and this result was remarkably consistent across sites and among children with different degrees of initial capability" (1972, p. 31).

Do we, however, know more about children now than we did 20 or 30 years ago? Do we know more about how they learn? Have we learned to measure the total impact of just going to school from grade to grade over a period of years? Do we know how children use the school experience in developing intellectual skills and in their social and emotional growth? Can we identify the effects of home experience on school performance? How does a child become the kind of student he will be?

These are rhetorical questions that have puzzled educators for generations. They are questions without definite answers, but their continuing challenge gave impetus to this longitudinal study.

The task of researchers carrying on longitudinal studies requires patience and longevity. The staff of this study was admirably endowed with the former and the writer blessed with the latter. Two other important and necessary assets were, however, missing—the availability of a wide variety of services, and guaranteed supporting funds for a reasonable period of time. This set of circumstances shaped a design that was to focus entirely on the school experience depending essentially on city-wide group tests, personal conversations with children, teachers, and parents, and upon observations of children as they moved through the grades on their journey through school. The emphasis was on the process of learning rather than on the act of teaching, a direction also advocated more recently by the Chancellor of the New York City school system (Scribner, 1971).

It might be helpful at this point to review the origin and development of this study. It was begun in 1952 by the New York City Board of Education in response to a request by the Superintendent of Schools that a study be made to measure the impact of the elementary school program upon the city's children and to evaluate its effectiveness.

As a result, representatives of most of the divisions and bureaus of the New York City Board of Education were called together to form a planning committee, and a staff of five teachers and a part-time director were selected to form the project staff. There followed a year of planning and orientation, the selection of a technical advisory committee of persons in and outside of the New York City school system, and an intensive period of orientation for the staff. In retrospect, the early activities and plans seem quite uncertain and confused, perhaps unavoidably so, because the mandate was so broad and undefined.

Children in five schools in New York City were selected for study and a staff member was assigned to each of them. Random selection of this combined school population would have been more representative of the one million children who attend the public schools in the city, but this was not possible. The intensity of the study that was envisaged required the active cooperation of teachers, principals, and field superintendents, and as a result, the schools selected were those where the opportunities for research and for study had the greatest potential. Nevertheless, an examination of the school population selected and the areas in which they were located revealed that they did provide a broad sampling which, although not random, was largely representative.

The very process of selection to assure the minimum conditions necessary for the success of a study precludes an absolute representative population and negates random sampling. Kagan and Moss speak of this problem and state, "Longitudinal samples are usually not representative" (1962, p. 4), and "assurance of a random sampling in a longitudinal program is . . . practically unattainable" (1962, p. 5).

From 1952 to 1953 much work was done in crystallizing methods of studying children, in devising scales, in determining what cooperation would be expected from teachers and what specific training they would need. In the fall of 1953 members of the staff entered their schools with detailed plans to study all children who had just entered the kindergarten. Visits to these schools had previously been made in the spring of that year during the registration period, and it was at this time that members of the staff assisted at school registration and had their first opportunity to meet both parents and children.

The year was hardly under way when serious problems of research arose. The goals of the study were not yet defined, and the requirement that the staff observe the impact of the school on children and at the same time evaluate the effectiveness of their education presented insurmountable problems.

Furthermore, the teachers in whose classes we were working were very much aware that we were also observing their teaching practices, a fact that resulted in teacher anxiety concerning the quality of their performance and a genuine eagerness for improvement. It should be emphasized that all teachers were carrying out desirable programs and that they were all able persons, functioning effectively. It was, perhaps, unrealistic to expect that there be any single program under way in all classrooms in the study. As can be seen more clearly in retrospect, *The Program* in one classroom might differ from that in a classroom directly across the hall, and *The Program* in one school might differ from that in another school. In fact, any slavish adherence on the part of teachers to any single detailed program would have given it a rigidity completely contradictory to the aims and to the philosophy of the elementary school program.

The results were inevitable. Although the staff spent considerable time in observing children and in training teachers for more effective observation of their children, they were being utilized increasingly as curriculum experts and in helping teachers to make curricular adaptations. The situation was further complicated by the schools' misunderstanding of the function of the project staff.

As the year ended, it became evident that the original aims of the study were not being fulfilled. A subcommittee of the planning committee was appointed with instructions to crystallize the aims of the study and to redirect and redesign its structure so that long-range goals could be achieved. As a result, the project was divided into two distinct studies. One sought to determine to what extent teachers were able to carry out and implement the program of elementary education; that is, how realistic was the program. This was to be achieved by visiting outstanding teachers in schools throughout the city who had been recommended by assistant superintendents in their school districts. These teachers were to be observed and interviewed about their work and their understanding of the program. It was envisaged that first-grade classes would be visited beginning in September 1954, second-grade classes in 1955, and each subsequent year would be devoted to visiting classes on the next higher grade until classes in all six grades had been observed. This study was completed in 1960, and a report of its findings was subsequently issued (New York City Board of Education, 1962).

It was further decided that the other aspect of the study was to be devoted to a long-range longitudinal study of certain groups of New York City children. This aspect was designed to study children as they were, to determine how children learn, how they feel, how they grow, how they adjust to typical school situations in which no effort is made to manipulate the environment or alter school procedures. To keep the two studies completely separate and to avoid further confusion, it was specifically agreed that the schools involved in the longitudinal study of children would not be included in the study of schools where outstanding teachers and promising practices would be sought. The project staff thus became responsible for two distinct and somewhat unrelated studies.

Unfortunately, the annual budgetary problems that beset the New York City Board of Education did not leave this project unscathed. At the end of the school year in June 1954, a full-time director was added to the staff, but three other staff positions were eliminated. As a result, three of the five schools had to be eliminated from the project, which found itself after one year with one full-time director (the writer), three full-time staff members, and two of the staff of the Bureau of Educational Research who were "on loan" for one day per week. It was not until the following year that the project was given the services of a part-time secretary.

Thus the redesigned project continued its study of the children as they entered the first grade of the remaining two schools in September 1954. One staff member, previously assigned to the school identified as the Jefferson School in this study, resumed her role there while the other two remained at the Washington School with its larger population. Plans were formulated to continue studying this group of children until they had completed the sixth grade in 1960.

With the completion of the report of teaching practices in 1960 and with a change in school superintendents, the school administration all but lost interest in the longitudinal study, but one staff position was continued until 1963. The writer remained as Director of the project but had already been given responsibility for the direction of a completely unrelated research project with a new staff.

Fortunately, all the children in the Jefferson School went on together into one junior high school, thus making it possible for the one remaining staff member, who had been with them throughout the elementary school years, to move with them and to maintain the continuity necessary in a longitudinal study. We were not as successful with the children in the Washington School. In an effort to achieve better racial integration, these children were divided among three neighboring junior high schools, and of necessity, the writer assumed responsibility for continuing data gathering for this group. It should be noted that school personnel were very cooperative but that frequent telephone calls and infrequent visits could not produce the rich quality of observations and conversations being gathered with the other group of children. Nevertheless, citywide testing programs and follow-up of specific children did provide sufficient group data for inclusion here.

When most of the children completed the ninth grade in 1963, all Board of Education support for the project ended. Although we were grateful that minimal support had been provided for three years beyond the original terminal date, the realization that the study had ended, that the data would probably be discarded, and that it would take another researcher 10 years to reach this point, was indeed traumatic.

It was just at this time that the writer resigned his Board of Education position as Project Director to join the faculty of Hunter College, and through the intervention of the assistant superintendent in charge of research, permission was granted to take all files and data with him to the college. The writer thus became the sole researcher in the subsequent years of this longitudinal study.

The three years that children in the study attended high school were difficult research years not only because of the complete absence of staff but also because of the dispersal of the children. When the Jefferson School children left their junior high school, they enrolled in 16 different New York City high schools, while the Washington School children, because of their location in a different borough of the city, began their tenth grade in 22 different high schools. (There were 86 high schools in New York City.) Contacts from that time on became limited to mailed questionnaires, telephone calls, and occasional visits to the few schools having a sizable number of these children.

The resulting attrition of subjects in the study was inevitable. Some did not answer requests for information, some were absent so much that the schools could give little information about their performance and progress, and others dropped out of school completely. Efforts to trace them were either rebuffed or unsuccessful. Nevertheless, a questionnaire mailed at their completion of the twelfth grade brought responses from 16 Washington School subjects and from 48 Jefferson School subjects. These, of course, were the children who had remained through graduation from high school. In general, children who were successful, especially from the Jefferson School, welcomed our inquiries, and up to this writing some spontaneously notify us of their progress, their marriages, and other changes in their personal lives.

By coincidence, four girls of the Jefferson School population and one boy from the Washington School subsequently enrolled in Hunter College, with which the writer is affiliated, thus providing frequent personal contacts and consultation, and many delightful nostalgic conversations about their childhood. Showing them their childhood writings and drawings was invariably a richly rewarding experience.

Most of the material described in this study is based on group data that were obtainable only from the kindergarten through the ninth grade, or up to the age of 14. Findings beyond that time are included where pertinent to specific individuals or in the chapter on conclusions. Several of the case studies presented are brought up to the present writing, when the subjects are approximately 25 years old.

Returning now to 1954, we find a redesigned longitudinal study of children who had entered the kindergartens of two New York City schools the previous year. The staff consisted of a full-time Director and three teachers who had been relieved of their classes to carry on the planned research. The previous year spent in the kindergartens of five schools had been of great value. In the two schools remaining in the project, sufficient data had been collected about the children to make their kindergarten year an integral part of the total study. Data gathered in the schools dropped from the project supplied interesting cross-sectional information and provided the material for a subsequent publication (New York City Board of Education, 1957) which outlined suggested orientation procedures for children newly enrolled in the early grades of school.

The thrust of the study was to present a school point of view of the consistency of behavior and performance. Of necessity, we were concerned with questions that teachers ask about children who just go to and from school every day without outside assistance or intervention.

What first-grade teacher has not looked at her children and longed for prescience to know whether the bright child would continue to show his superiority, whether the dull were doomed to continue this pattern throughout their schooling, whether the slow reader would be a late bloomer or would always be a slow reader, whether the maladjusted child was merely going through a period of initial difficulty or whether he was showing the symptoms of more serious and more permanent maladjustment. Upper-grade teachers have asked similar questions when assessing the strengths and weaknesses of their junior high school pupils. "When did Alice first begin to write so creatively? When was her talent discovered?" "When did Robert's reading difficulties begin? Was he always reading below grade level?" "When was Lucy first identified as a behavior problem?" School records may provide quantitative but rarely qualitative answers to such questions.

To increase understanding of these problems, the study was designed to answer questions such as the following:

Are there discernible patterns in children's learning processes?

How early does the level of achievement become fixed?

How do current practices of retention and acceleration affect children?

How early is the promise of giftedness identified?

To what extent do traumatic experiences affect learning and adjustment?

How early are serious symptoms of maladjustment displayed?

What is the significance of "separation-from-parent" anxiety and school phobia when starting school?

What is the effect of mobility upon learning and adjustment?

In answering these and similar questions it was hoped that data might be collected which would provide perspective to look back, to identify symptoms of disturbances, and also to note encouraging predictors of achievement and success.

Examination of the research showed that most studies of children were cross-sectional, revealing a present status or condition; longitudinal studies were very few, though badly needed.

The statements frequently heard that there is insufficient research . . . are well grounded. The greatest need, no doubt, is for carefully documented longitudinal studies on all aspects of child development [U.S. Dept. HEW, 1958, p. 198].

Scarvia B. Anderson, director of an eight-year study for the Educational Testing Service, states:

Relatively few large-scale educational studies have traced the same individuals over a period of time. Inferences about growth which have been made from "cross-sectional" or status studies (testing different grades at the same time) have often proved misleading [Anderson, 1961, p. 1].

Lavin writes:

. . . More longitudinal studies are needed . . . we are ignorant regarding the consistency of performance and the degree to which it is predictable over time [1965, p. 58].

Bloom also discusses the need and the distinct advantages of longitudinal studies and speculates about the dearth of such research:

The length of time required for longitudinal studies and the tremendous cost of such studies probably account for the relatively small number of such investigations. With a few notable exceptions, the person responsible for setting up the study is rarely available to complete it. All too frequently, someone else was employed at the end of the study to process the data and write up the results.

In addition to time and cost, the repetitive nature of the data collecting process and the extreme amount of administrative and clerical energy required to maintain contact with the subjects and keep the records in good condition are all sources of discouragement in longitudinal research [1964, p. 224].

The better known longitudinal studies present, for the most part, the results of research in physical growth, mental growth, personality development, or a combination of these. Furthermore, investigators in these studies had easy access to homes, to parents, and to other nonschool aspects of the child's total environment. Some of these studies began in early infancy and continued into the primary-grade years. Others trace the growth of their subjects from early adolescence into adulthood.

Probably the earliest and the classic in longitudinal studies is Terman's Genetic Studies of Genius (Terman et al., 1925; Burks, Jensen, and Terman, 1930; Terman and Oden, 1947, 1959). In 1921 Terman identified approximately 1500 children in California with IQ's over 135. This group, who are now more than 60 years old, has been studied intensively for more than 40 years (Oden, 1968) with measures of intelligence and achievement, with medical examinations, batteries of inventories, questionnaires, and character tests. This study indicates that the early promise of giftedness is fulfilled in adult life and negates the stereotype of the gifted person as a maladjusted individual with severe personal problems.

Of equal distinction have been the Gesell studies at the Yale Clinic of Child Development carried on over varying periods of time (1926, 1928, 1940; Gesell et al., 1937, 1939, 1941, 1943, 1946, 1947, 1956). These studies have had a tremendous impact upon our knowledge of child development.

Longitudinal studies conducted since 1929 by the Fels Research Institute for the Study of Human Development began in infancy with the children of families living in the area of the Institute. Children were observed at home, at the Institute, and in school and rich data were derived concerning mental growth and personality development (Sontag, Baker, and Nelson, 1958).

The California Growth Studies is an umbrella title covering the Berkeley Growth Study, the Berkeley Guidance Study, and the Oakland Study. These studies conducted intensive research with a wide range of measurements of physical and mental growth, personality development, social behavior, and familial factors which influenced these from infancy. Findings have been reported extensively (Bayley, 1933, 1940, 1949, 1955, 1964, 1968; Jones and Bayley, 1941; MacFarlane, 1964; Bayley and Schafer, 1964; Bronson, 1969).

The Harvard Growth Studies (Dearborn, Rothney, and Shuttleworth, 1938) carried on anthropometric measurements over a 35-year period and focused on nutritional, dental, and physical development. The University of Minnesota's Institute of Child Development and Welfare, using personality and adjustment inventories, was concerned with children's adjustment (Anderson et al., 1959); Thomas, Chess, and Birch's (1968) longitudinal study began in early infancy with studies of family patterns and behavioral traits of children.

Havighurst's longitudinal study of a postwar generation in "River City" was carried on from 1951 to 1960. The study began with 11-year-olds in the sixth grade and closed when most of them were 20. "They were studied as they studied, played, and worked in the schools, churches, homes, and shops of the community" (Havighurst et al., 1962, p. vii).

Kagan and Moss studied the personality development of 89 children taken from the Fels Research Institute longitudinal population and present the results of tests, observations, and interviews from the subject's birth to 29 years of age. Their study "is concerned primarily with the stability of selected motive-related behaviors, sources of anxiety, defensive responses and modes of interpersonal interaction from earliest childhood through young adulthood" (Kagan and Moss, 1962, p. 9).

The Menninger Foundation Study was concerned with 60 children who were not studied continuously but only at critical periods in their lives—infancy, preschool, childhood, and prepuberty. Factors related to continuity and to change were sought (Murphy, 1964).

Other major longitudinal studies that secured a large variety of personality and other measurements of children's growth are the Iowa Studies (Baldwin, 1921), the Chicago Study (Freeman and Flory, 1937), the Brush Foundation Study (Ebert and Simons, 1943), and Shirley's extensive studies of infants' growth and development (1933, 1938, 1939, 1941, 1942).

Finally, the Educational Testing Service of Princeton, New Jersey, is currently conducting its "ETS-Head Start Longitudinal Study of Disadvantaged Children and Their First School Experiences," which is scheduled to cover the years 1969–1974, that is, children from age 3 to grade 3. "The aims of the study are to identify the components of early education that are associated with children's development, determine the environmental and background factors that influence such associations, and, if possible, describe how these influences operate" (Anderson, 1969, p. 27).

All subjects in the longitudinal studies described were the beneficiaries of special interest, extensive out-of-school services and intervention in their rearing or in their school progress. The vast number of children who attend schools in America are not as fortunate, and perhaps the fact-finding approach of our study gives us some information about such children.

Furthermore, many of the children involved in this study would not have been included in other longitudinal studies because neither they nor their parents were able to sustain the interest and cooperation necessary for more extensive research. From a longitudinal point of view, this is a study of an unstudied population of children who form the majority of those found in our classrooms. In addition to its findings, its contribution to studies of child development may be in the direction of pointing up Bloom's (1964) observations concerning the need for better school cumulative records and the tremendous potentials such records would offer for longitudinal studies.

# CHAPTER TWO

## The Children

Although it is recognized that the results of a study of children in only two schools may not be applicable to all New York City school children, these schools were, nevertheless, sufficiently different in character and location so that they represented a picture of two broad segments of the school population.

One school that was retained in the study is located in the borough of Brooklyn, where it drew most of its children from a low middle-income housing project. Parents here were white-collar workers, skilled laborers, civil service employees, and a few were in business or members of a profession. Most of the children in this school went home for lunch and, as was to be expected, only one or two qualified for inclusion in the free lunch program. This school is referred to here as the Jefferson School. All of its children moved on to the same junior high school.

The other school is located in the upper part of Manhattan on the fringe of Harlem. The occupation of the parents of children in this school ranged from unskilled laborers to varying degrees of skilled laborers with a very few in the business and professional groups. Although the community was not classified among those on the lowest socioeconomic level, the school did draw most of its children from depressed areas. During their seven years in the elementary school, one-third of the approximately

1500 children were able to qualify for free lunch. Approximately 85% of the kindergarten and first-grade class was black; this same ratio continued from 1953 through 1963 when the children completed the junior high school grades. In an effort to create better integrated schools, these children had been dispersed among three junior high schools at the end of the sixth grade. Data for them, although increasingly more difficult to obtain, are shown in tables under their school of origin. For purposes of this study, this school is referred to as the Washington School.

Table 2-1 presents the ethnic distribution of these children using official classifications of New York City pupil population surveys. The term "basic" refers to the research population who remained with us at least through the ninth grade. Tables are presented to parallel the chronological order of observations.

**Table 2-1    Basic Population—Ethnic Origin**

| Ethnic Group | Jefferson School | | | Washington School | | |
|---|---|---|---|---|---|---|
| | Boys | Girls | Total | Boys | Girls | Total |
| Black | 5 | 2 | 7 | 26 | 43 | 69 |
| Hispanic | 1 | 0 | 1 | 2 | 1 | 3 |
| Others | 40 | 37 | 77 | 4 | 4 | 8 |
| Total | 46 | 39 | 85 | 32 | 48 | 80 |

Since attendance in kindergarten was not compulsory, the number of children admitted into the kindergartens of schools was determined basically by the number of places available. This presented no problem in the Jefferson School where there were a sufficient number of classes for those who applied. In the Washington School, however, with its larger population, there were many children who applied for admission to the kindergarten for whom no facilities were available. No such problem existed the following year in the first grade where, in accordance with state law, all applicants for admission had to be accepted. There were thus 246 children registered in the kindergartens of both schools, and 274 children on register at the end of the first grade, of whom 180 had been with us since entering kindergarten.

The decrease in population in the Jefferson School shown in Table 2-2 can be accounted for by the fact that 17 children moved out of the neighborhood during the kindergarten or first-grade years and were therefore lost to the study. In the Washington School, much greater attrition occurred during these first two years. The children who remained in these schools and who were to form our basic research population progressed through the grades in accordance with the following calendar:

ELEMENTARY SCHOOL

| | |
|---|---|
| 1953–1954 | Kindergarten |
| 1954–1955 | First grade |
| 1955–1956 | Second grade |
| 1956–1957 | Third grade |
| 1957–1958 | Fourth grade |
| 1958–1959 | Fifth grade |
| 1959–1960 | Sixth grade |

JUNIOR HIGH SCHOOL

| | |
|---|---|
| 1960–1961 | Seventh grade |
| 1961–1962 | Eighth grade |
| 1962–1963 | Ninth grade* |

SENIOR HIGH SCHOOL

| | |
|---|---|
| 1963–1964 | Tenth grade |
| 1964–1965 | Eleventh grade |
| 1965–1966 | Twelfth grade |

* Those who had been placed in special progress (SP) classes completed the ninth grade in 1962.

Table 2-2    Enrollment Summary

| | Kindergarten Register | | | First-Grade Register | | | In Study: Kindergarten and First Grade | | |
|---|---|---|---|---|---|---|---|---|---|
| | Boys | Girls | Total | Boys | Girls | Total | Boys | Girls | Total |
| Jefferson | 69 | 63 | 132 | 64 | 51 | 115 | 60 | 46 | 106 |
| Washington | 55 | 59 | 114 | 74 | 85 | 159 | 34 | 40 | 74 |
| Total | 124 | 122 | 246 | 138 | 136 | 274 | 94 | 86 | 180 |

The study group of children represents an age range smaller than any class before or after it. These children entered the kindergarten in September 1953 immediately after the age of admission in New York City had been raised from 4 years, 4 months to 4 years, 8 months. As a result, they ranged in age from 4 years, 8 months to 5 years, 3 months in the kindergarten and from 5 years, 8 months to 6 years, 3 months in the first grade, and so on—a range of 8 months instead of the usual 12. This group, then, was unique in that the age range in any one grade was less than one year throughout its schooling.

Although the project staff began gathering a variety of data early in the kindergarten year, it was not until the end of the first grade that an objective measurement of intelligence was used. At that time, all first-grade classes in New York City were given the Pinter-Cunningham Intelligence Test. This provided a general assessment of the school population, as well as the first measurement of individual potential. Table 2-3 shows how scores were distributed in the two schools for the *total* first-grade population of which the children who were to become basic formed a part.

Table 2-3  Distribution of IQ Scores—First Grade
Pinter-Cunningham Intelligence Test

| IQ | Jefferson School | | | Washington School | | |
|---|---|---|---|---|---|---|
| | Boys | Girls | Total | Boys | Girls | Total |
| 160–169 | 0 | 1 | 1 | 0 | 0 | 0 |
| 150–159 | 0 | 1 | 1 | 0 | 0 | 0 |
| 140–149 | 6 | 3 | 9 | 0 | 0 | 0 |
| 130–139 | 3 | 1 | 4 | 2 | 1 | 3 |
| 120–129 | 11 | 12 | 23 | 1 | 5 | 6 |
| 110–119 | 18 | 11 | 29 | 12 | 9 | 21 |
| 100–109 | 16 | 13 | 29 | 12 | 17 | 29 |
| 90–99 | 9 | 7 | 16 | 18 | 26 | 44 |
| 80–89 | 5 | 5 | 10 | 22 | 15 | 37 |
| 70–79 | 0 | 0 | 0 | 7 | 6 | 13 |
| 60–69 | 0 | 0 | 0 | 1 | 2 | 3 |
| Total [a] | 68 | 54 | 122 | 75 | 81 | 156 |
| Range | | | 81–164 | | | 62–139 |
| Median | | | 114 | | | 94 |
| Mean | | | 113.0 | | | 96.11 |

[a] Excludes children in Washington School not tested because of language difficulties.

## THE BASIC POPULATION

It would have been unrealistic to expect that the 278 children in the first grade and the additional 20 who were admitted in the second grade would all remain in their original elementary schools through the sixth grade and would be available for study through the ninth grade. In fact, the selection of the Washington School population for intensive study was questioned by those who knew of the school's high mobility rate. It was therefore very gratifying to find that 85 (70%) of the original 122 children in the Jefferson School remained to complete the sixth grade, as did 80 of the 172 (47%) in the Washington School. Moreover, 80 of the former and 68 of the latter completed the ninth grade in junior high schools accessible to the project staff. Longitudinal data for the elementary school years was thus available for the 165 children who formed our basic group, while 148 of these were studied through the ninth grade. Data were recorded for 85 of our children who were graduated from high school, although only 64 responded to our questionnaire at that time. Table 2-4 incorporates these data.

Table 2-4  Basic Population Attrition

| | Jefferson School | | | Washington School | | |
|---|---|---|---|---|---|---|
| | Boys | Girls | Total | Boys | Girls | Total |
| Elementary school | | | | | | |
| First grade | 64 | 51 | 115 | 74 | 85 | 159 |
| Sixth grade | 46 | 39 | 85 | 32 | 48 | 80 |
| Junior high school | | | | | | |
| Ninth-grade two-year SP program | 17 | 15 | 32 | 2 | 5 | 7 |
| Ninth-grade three-year program | 25 | 23 | 48 | 24 | 37 | 61 |
| Total graduates | 42 | 38 | 80 | 26 | 42 | 68 |
| Senior high school graduates | 33 | 27 | 60 | 12 | 13 | 25 |

Basic children were found in all classes of each grade in their schools and at no time was any attempt made to isolate them. Children who were newly admitted during the course of each year to classes on the grade then under study were treated as if they were part of the basic group and were involved in all tests, questionnaires, and observations that were being carried on. These nonbasic children who were with us anywhere from a few weeks to a few years provided valuable additional data that were used for purposes of comparison and for the observation of processes and patterns of large groups of a given grade or school. As a result, the study entailed contact during the seven-year elementary school period with approximately 1000 children. Of these only 165 remained for at least five years and eventually constituted the basic re-

**Table 2-5  Grade Registers** [a]

| | Jefferson School | | | | | | Washington School | | | | | |
|---|---|---|---|---|---|---|---|---|---|---|---|---|
| | Total Group | | | Basic Group | | | Total Group | | | Basic Group | | |
| Grade | Boys | Girls | Total | Boys | Girls | Total | Boys | Girls | Total | Boys | Girls | Total |
| K | 69 | 63 | 132 | 38 | 31 | 69 | 55 | 59 | 114 | 18 | 28 | 46 |
| 1 | 64 | 51 | 115 | 43 | 35 | 78 | 74 | 85 | 159 | 26 | 41 | 67 |
| 2 | 64 | 51 | 115 | 46 | 39 | 85 | 93 | 106 | 199 | 32 | 48 | 80 |
| 3 | 60 | 49 | 109 | 46 | 39 | 85 | 96 | 104 | 200 | 32 | 48 | 80 |
| 4 | 60 | 52 | 112 | 46 | 39 | 85 | 91 | 102 | 193 | 32 | 48 | 80 |
| 5 | 59 | 49 | 108 | 46 | 39 | 85 | 96 | 108 | 204 | 32 | 48 | 80 |
| 6 | 52 | 47 | 99 | 46 | 39 | 85 | 89 | 111 | 200 | 32 | 48 | 80 |

[a] Total junior high school grade registers were unavailable.

search population. It should be emphasized here that trends observed were frequently studied not only with our nonbasic children but also in other schools of similar populations.

Table 2-5 indicates the number of pupils on register in each of the grades through which our children progressed. Among them were those who were destined to remain in the school and to become part of the basic group. Since no new children were included in the basic population after the second grade, figures for this group become fixed at this point.

It might be valuable, at this point, to examine our basic children more closely. Their ethnic background has been given in Table 2-1. When did they first enter our schools? From what backgrounds did they come? These questions can be answered succinctly by Tables 2-6 and 2-7.

**Table 2-6    Basic Population—Grade of Entry into Study Group**

| Grade | Jefferson School | | | Washington School | | |
|---|---|---|---|---|---|---|
| | Boys | Girls | Total | Boys | Girls | Total |
| K | 38 | 31 | 69 | 18 | 28 | 46 |
| 1 | 5 | 4 | 9 | 8 | 13 | 21 |
| 2 | 3 | 4 | 7 | 6 | 7 | 13 |
| Total | 46 | 39 | 85 | 32 | 48 | 80 |

Figures in Table 2-7 indicate the number of children who entered the school as only children, or with one or more than one younger or older sibling in the family. These figures changed during the course of the study as siblings were born.

Information was also gathered concerning "disrupted" homes— homes with one parent or a stepparent. "Disrupted" here refers only to the disruption of the original parent relationship by death, separation, or divorce. Here, too, the family constellation changed for many children during the progress of the study.

It should be emphasized that no inferences or conclusions are being drawn from the presence or absence of "disrupted" homes. For some children, the sheer attrition of marital discord was far more traumatic than the act of separation. It should further be pointed out that some of our children who are included in this category were the recipients of as much concern, affection, and security as they could possibly have received in a home with two natural parents. Table 2-8 gives quantitative data concerning such known "disrupted" homes that existed at the time of the entrance of our basic children into school. It is presented with the full

**Table 2-7  Basic Population—Ordinal Position in Family at Time of Admission**

| Ordinal Position | Jefferson School | | | | | | | | | Washington School | | | | | | | | |
|---|---|---|---|---|---|---|---|---|---|---|---|---|---|---|---|---|---|---|
| | Younger Siblings in Family | | | | | | | | | Younger Siblings in Family | | | | | | | | |
| | None | | | One | | | More Than One | | | None | | | One | | | More Than One | | |
| | Boys | Girls | Total | Boys | Girls | Total | Boys | Girls | Total | Boys | Girls | Total | Boys | Girls | Total | Boys | Girls | Total |
| Only child | 7 | 9 | 16 | | | | | | | 8 | 8 | 16 | | | | | | |
| First child | | | | 24 | 14 | 38 | 4 | 1 | 5 | 0 | 1 | 1 | 6 | 8 | 14 | 2 | 5 | 7 |
| Second child | 9 | 12 | 21 | 1 | 1 | 2 | 0 | 1 | 1 | 3 | 6 | 9 | 5 | 4 | 9 | 1 | 1 | 2 |
| Third child | 1 | 1 | 2 | | | | | | | 2 | 3 | 5 | 1 | 2 | 3 | 1 | 2 | 3 |
| Fourth child | | | | | | | | | | 1 | 1 | 2 | 0 | 0 | 0 | 0 | 2 | 2 |
| Fifth child | | | | | | | | | | | | | 0 | 1 | 1 | | | |
| Sixth child | | | | | | | | | | 1 | 1 | 2 | 0 | 2 | 2 | | | |
| Seventh child | | | | | | | | | | | | | | | | | | |
| Eighth child | | | | | | | | | | 0 | 1 | 1 | | | | | | |
| Ninth child | | | | | | | | | | | | | | | | | | |
| Tenth child | | | | | | | | | | | | | | | | | | |
| Eleventh child | | | | | | | | | | 1 | 0 | 1 | | | | | | |
| Total [a] | 17 | 22 | 39 | 25 | 15 | 40 | 4 | 2 | 6 | 16 | 21 | 37 | 12 | 17 | 29 | 4 | 10 | 14 |

[a] Includes second-grade admissions.

19

realization that some of the data may be erroneous or incomplete because such situations were not always revealed. Information concerning this factor became increasingly difficult to obtain during the junior high school years when fewer contacts with parents and children were possible.

Table 2-8    Basic Population—Incidence of "Disrupted" Homes at Beginning and End of Elementary School

|  | Jefferson School | | | Washington School | | |
|  | Boys | Girls | Total | Boys | Girls | Total |
|---|---|---|---|---|---|---|
| Grade 1 | 0 | 0 | 0 | 5 | 19 | 24 |
| Grade 6 [a] | 1 | 2 | 3 | 11 | 19 | 30 |
| Basic $N$ | 46 | 39 | 85 | 32 | 48 | 80 |

[a] Figures include disrupted homes shown in Grade 1.

Finally, what potential, as measured by the first group intelligence test, did our basic children show? Table 2-9 shows the distribution of IQ scores for children who became our basic population. These scores have previously been included in Table 2-3, which shows scores of the total first-grade group.

Table 2-9    Distribution of Basic Group Scores—First Grade Pintner-Cunningham Intelligence Test

|  | Jefferson School | | | Washington School | | |
| IQ | Boys | Girls | Total | Boys | Girls | Total |
|---|---|---|---|---|---|---|
| 160–169 | 0 | 1 | 1 | 0 | 0 | 0 |
| 150–159 | 0 | 1 | 1 | 0 | 0 | 0 |
| 140–149 | 4 | 2 | 6 | 0 | 0 | 0 |
| 130–139 | 2 | 0 | 2 | 0 | 0 | 0 |
| 120–129 | 7 | 8 | 15 | 1 | 4 | 5 |
| 110–119 | 12 | 11 | 23 | 9 | 5 | 14 |
| 100–109 | 10 | 6 | 16 | 7 | 9 | 16 |
| 90–99 | 8 | 6 | 14 | 7 | 18 | 25 |
| 80–89 | 3 | 4 | 7 | 5 | 8 | 13 |
| 70–79 | 0 | 0 | 0 | 2 | 3 | 5 |
| 60–69 | 0 | 0 | 0 | 1 | 1 | 2 |
| Total | 46 | 39 | 85 | 32 | 48 | 80 |
| Range | 84–146 | 82–164 | 82–164 | 66–120 | 66–126 | 66–126 |
| Mean | 112.2 | 112.7 | 112.5 | 100.8 | 97.1 | 98.6 |

# CHAPTER THREE

## Learning About Our Children—THE INSTRUMENTS

As in most studies of this kind, there was much anxiety that data that had not been anticipated might subsequently be needed. There was a sense of urgency to leave no aspect of growth unrecorded, even though it was acknowledged that some might not be needed.

Standardized tests were available for measuring achievement and intelligence. The measurement of behavior and personality traits was much more difficult. Many published scales were examined, but few were applicable to our population or warranted the time required for their use. Original scales and questionnaires were therefore devised which were thought to be simpler and which subsequently proved to provide significant information.

In selecting tests for measuring achievement, an attempt was made to use, wherever possible, those that were being administered on a city-wide basis. In the grades not included in the general testing program, supplementary achievement tests were administered by the project staff. The following standardized tests were used:

## For Measuring Achievement

### Reading

The New York Reading Readiness Test (Grade 1)
New York Test of Growth in Reading (Grade 2)
Gates Primary Reading Test—Type 3 (Grade 2)
Metropolitan Achievement Tests—Primary, Elementary, Intermediate and Advanced (Grades 3–9)
Stanford Achievement Test—Intermediate (Grade 5)

### Mathematics

N.Y. Inventory of Mathematical Concepts (Grades 1, 2, 3, 4, and 5)
Metropolitan Achievement Tests—Intermediate (Grade 6)

## For Measuring Intelligence

Pintner-Cunningham Primary Test (Grade 1)
Otis Quick Scoring Mental Ability Tests—Alpha (Grade 3)
Otis Quick Scoring Mental Ability Tests—Beta (Grade 6)
Pintner General Ability Test (Grade 9)
Wechsler Intelligence Scale for Children
Revised Stanford-Binet Intelligence Scale
Henmon-Nelson Tests of Mental Ability

It was hoped that during the next few years we could obtain individual IQ scores for each of our children. This proved to be an illusion and although local colleges were most cooperative, less than half the children could be examined. Individual Wechsler and Binet IQ scores are shown wherever available and pertinent to the discussion. The Henmon-Nelson Test was administered only to children whose teachers had recommended them for admission to Special Progress classes in junior high school but whose IQ scores were below the required minimum.

## For Assessing Behavior and Personality

Haggerty-Olson-Wickman Behavior Rating Schedules
California Test of Personality
Ohio Social Acceptance Scale

The Haggerty-Olson-Wickman Behavior Schedule was used with only a few classes but was abandoned as being too cumbersome and imposing too much on teachers' time. Another research project under way in the Jefferson School utilized the Ohio Social Acceptance Scale, the results of which were given to us. All of these scales were used only once and furnished little information that was not already becoming available through our own original scales and questionnaires which were designed to guide the project staff and teachers in their observations of children and to obtain information in their study of child growth. These instruments were tested and refined to meet the following criteria:

> They were to supply information about each child that could be obtained in no other way.
> They must in no way threaten the teacher.
> They must impose little or no clerical burden upon the teacher.
> They must be easy to use.

The following rating scales (see Appendix) were thus devised:

> Teacher's Estimate of Reading Development—to determine each child's achievement and interest in reading, as judged by the teacher.
>
> Teacher's Estimate of Intelligence—to determine each child's level of potential as estimated by the teacher.
>
> Attitude Toward Classroom Activity—to measure children's reactions to, and participation in classroom activity.
>
> General Adjustment Rating Scale—to note the extent of behavioral adjustment of each child, and to record teachers' recommendations for special services where indicated.

These are described more fully in the pages following. In addition to scores from standardized intelligence and achievement tests, the following were gathered for all children:

*From children*

Samples of drawings and paintings—Twice each year, children drew or painted for the Project Assistants a picture of "yourself," of "a person," of "your family," and of "anything." For some children, the self-portraits and family portraits provided interesting supplementary personality data. This material was also used for comparison with the drawings of children two decades later. The changes are reported in Chapter Nine.

Samples of handwriting—It was hoped that these would provide a record of the development of muscular coordination. Children were asked to use their best handwriting in writing on the following topics:

Grade 3—If I Had $10
Grade 4—The Most Fun I Ever Had
Grade 5—If I Could Fly
Grade 6—If I Were a Teacher

In Grades 1 and 2, sentences were copied from the chalkboard. Handwriting itself proved to have no significance and in no case were there any radical unexpected changes. With all children, fine muscular coordination improved with physical maturity. The writing content, however, was frequently fascinating, as the samples given in Chapter Eight indicate.

Children's questionnaires—These were devised to obtain reactions and attitudes of children toward various phases of their school environment as well as their personal lives. Until reading and writing ceased to be a problem, the questions were read orally by the project staff members in individual conferences with children and their answers were recorded. For the most part, the same questions were used on each subsequent questionnaire.

Sociometric measures—These measures were based upon responses to the following questions:

Grade 1—Whom would you like to sit next to?
Grade 2—Whom would you like to sit next to?
Grade 3—Whom would you like for your partner on class trips?
Grade 4—If you could choose anyone in the class, a boy or a girl, as a partner for a class trip, whom would you choose?
Grade 5—If you had your choice, which child of your class would you like to have with you in your class next September? If you couldn't get this one, whom would you choose second? third?
In the fifth grade the Ohio Social Acceptance Scale was used along with the sociogram. This scale endeavors to determine not only the degree to which a child is accepted by his classmates but the extent to which he reaches out and seeks their friendship.
Grade 6—If you could choose, which boy or girl in your present class would you like to have in your class in junior high school? If you couldn't have this child, whom would you choose second? third? If you are eager to add more names you may do so in order of your choice.

## From Parents

Parent questionnaires—These were designed to provide background information as well as to indicate parental attitudes toward the schools.

Parent interviews—Supplementary data were supplied by the parents who requested interviews with project staff members. In the early grades, a large number of parents in both schools requested such interviews. As a result, excellent relationships were developed between the project staff and the many parents who sought a nonauthoritative figure who was connected with the school but who was not one of its faculty.

## From Teachers

After orientation conferences with Project Assistants, teachers prepared the following data:

Teacher judgment of readiness in areas listed on the New York Reading Readiness Test—This scale is part of the New York Reading Readiness Test and was used only in the first grade before formal reading instruction had been begun.

Teacher's Estimate of Reading Development—This scale proved to be less reliable than the achievement tests. Teachers frequently estimated the reading levels of their pupils in terms of the basic reader which they were using and where the level of the reader used was limited to that of the grade, the true ceiling of children's abilities was rarely identified. Average or poor readers were more often correctly identified than were the superior readers. Nevertheless, this scale frequently provided insights into the standards that teachers used in evaluating pupil progress.

Teacher's Estimate of Intelligence—This scale was, of course, of most value before the first intelligence test had been given in the first grade. However, after IQ scores were available, many teachers were still able to sense abilities that were not supported by IQ scores, whose validity they questioned. This independence of teachers in judging intelligence frequently gave clues to disparities between performance and IQs and suggested children who warranted closer observation and study.

Attitude Toward Classroom Activity—This scale indicated, for the most part, the close relationship between ability and interest.

General Adjustment Rating Scale—This was a five-point scale on which teachers rated each child's behavioral adjustment. This scale consistently proved to be of great value.

Lists of children with adjustment problems—These were obtained twice a year, once in November and once in March. One of the purposes here was to provide teachers with spaced opportunities to identify their problem children and to discuss them with the project staff.

Lists of gifted and talented children—These were obtained each year in an effort to determine how early and how frequently the promise of superior potential was identified.

For certain children the following data were gathered:

Anecdotal material—Anecdotal records were at first kept for a random sampling of 25 children in each of the two schools. These children had been selected in the kindergarten. However, after the second year of the study, it was felt that time could more profitably be spent in keeping detailed anecdotal records for all those children whose behavior or learning patterns warranted it. Such records were kept throughout the period of the study.

Notations for deviates—All children were regularly observed but notations were made for those who showed deviations in physical, emotional, social, or intellectual growth. For example, continuous records were kept for the tallest children, the shortest children, left-handed children, and all who showed noticeable deviations from the norm.

Other data—Other data that were gathered included copies of school records, health and test cards, and pertinent health information that was supplied by nurses and doctors.

Notes concerning the socioeconomic background of each of the two school communities, their resources, and changing patterns were recorded.

The excellent relationships that developed between project staff members and their schools, their children, and parents facilitated the gathering of information and helped immeasurably in obtaining enthusiastic cooperation. Two staff members or Project Assistants, as they became known, were assigned to the larger Washington School and one to the Jefferson School, where they spent approximately three days a week. As children progressed each year from grade to grade, and teacher to teacher, Project Assistants moved with them. Although great care was taken never to interfere with school procedures or school placement, it cannot be denied that the presence of the Project Assistants and the halo effect of the study produced some intervention and was probably of great value to a number of children. However, the study could not have been carried on had these relationships not developed.

The project was very fortunate in being provided with substitute teachers who were sent into classrooms to relieve regular teachers with whom individual conferences had been scheduled. The freedom from tension and anxiety that this gave teachers was of enormous value to Project Assistants, who conferred with each of the teachers of our children for approximately two hours a month. Teachers also were eager for these conferences in which they could discuss their children and be helped to gain valuable insights. These sessions provided priceless opportunities for learning about the children and for orienting teachers to the purposes of the study and to the use of the scales that had been provided.

Before a new scale was introduced, discussion was directed by the Project Assistants to the purposes of the scale and to the meanings of words. For example, before teachers were asked to complete the General Adjustment Rating Scale, the meaning of adjustment in the school situation was discussed. Teachers were encouraged to give their own interpretations in these discussions and to apply them to specific children in their classes. These discussions aimed to make certain that teacher and Project Assistant agreed on the interpretation of the material and hence that data obtained from teachers had greater reliability and validity.

Not all scales turned out to have equal value for the study nor were all data usable. In fact, far more data were gathered than could possibly be used or interpreted. It is therefore interesting to note that with the exception of data connected with the beginning of reading, all scales and materials planned for use during the first year of the study were found to be sufficiently valuable to warrant their continuation throughout the course of the study. As indicated earlier, the only important change was in reporting anecdotal material, and only the focus was changed there.

# CHAPTER FOUR

## The Learning Process

**INTELLIGENCE**

In accordance with the practices of the New York City school system then in effect, our basic children were given intelligence tests in the first, third, sixth, and eighth grades. Scores on the Pinter-Cunningham Primary Test given in the first grade, which have already been presented, are included in Table 4-1 along with a description of scores subsequently obtained on intelligence tests given in the third, sixth, and eighth grades.

Inspection of mean group IQ scores reveals a remarkable consistency between first-, sixth-, and eighth-grade scores in the Jefferson School and among mean scores on all four tests in the Washington School. Only on the Otis Alpha test in the Jefferson School was there a considerable variation from previous and subsequent means.

The selection of valid tests for New York City's heterogeneous population presents a baffling problem. It is well known that tests become less reliable in measuring the upper and lower intellectual levels of the school population than they are in measuring the average. Some tests seem to have greater validity and reliability for the middle and upper portion of the population, whereas others are useful for the lower and middle groups. Citywide experience seems to indicate that the Otis Alpha

**Table 4-1  Description of IQ Scores**

| Test | | Jefferson School | | | Washington School | | |
|---|---|---|---|---|---|---|---|
| | | $N$ [a] | Mean | Standard Deviation | $N$ [a] | Mean | Standard Deviation |
| Pintner-Cunningham Primary, Grade 1 | Boys | 46 | 112.24 | 15.57 | 32 | 100.78 | 14.97 |
| | Girls | 39 | 112.74 | 17.99 | 48 | 97.13 | 13.31 |
| | Total | 85 | 112.46 | 16.74 | 80 | 98.59 | 14.11 |
| Otis Quick-Scoring Alpha, Grade 3 | Boys | 46 | 103.74 | 12.18 | 32 | 96.78 | 11.76 |
| | Girls | 39 | 104.21 | 12.33 | 47 | 95.19 | 11.09 |
| | Total | 85 | 103.95 | 12.30 | 79 | 95.84 | 11.35 |
| Otis Quick-Scoring Mental Ability Beta, Grade 6 | Boys | 44 | 114.89 | 17.06 | 32 | 95.66 | 13.51 |
| | Girls | 39 | 109.90 | 12.74 | 48 | 98.46 | 12.14 |
| | Total | 83 | 112.54 | 15.43 | 80 | 97.34 | 12.86 |
| Pintner General Ability Intermediate, Grade 8 [b] | Boys | 32 | 118.96 | 16.98 | 21 | 94.38 | 14.48 |
| | Girls | 32 | 112.56 | 12.29 | 35 | 98.83 | 16.59 |
| | Total | 64 | 115.76 | 16.89 | 56 | 97.16 | 15.90 |

[a] Decrease in $N$ indicates loss of children to the study in the junior high school years or missing scores.
[b] Special Progress children were given test in Grade 9.

test is more reliable for lower groups because of its low ceiling, and as a result, brighter children in most schools achieve lower scores on this intelligence test than on any other. This may account for the variation in mean IQ scores in the Jefferson School.

Much has been said and written recently about the "deterioration of IQs" among underprivileged children (Shuey, 1958; Osborne, 1960; Stein and Susser, 1970). It should be emphasized that an IQ score is not an absolute measure of potential and is greatly influenced by the items and construction of a particular test. Furthermore, since different intelligence tests measure different samples of skills which are thought to be aspects of the total capacity to learn, some changes in IQs should be expected from test to test and accepted far more readily than they are by both educators and laymen. "If we look inside the tests, it should be obvious that the kinds of learnings we typically appraise at the earlier ages bear little resemblance, and may have little relevance, to the kinds of learnings we appraise later" (Wesman, 1968, p. 271). Chauncey and Dobbin point out: "No intelligence test opens a window in the student's skull through which psychologists can ascertain the amount of latent brightness or intelligence he has. . . . A rough appraisal of the individual's *comparative* capacity for learning is the most that the best test of intelligence can provide" (1963, p. 21).

When one speaks of the deterioration of the IQ, there is an implied assumption concerning the reliability of the first IQ score. There is no evidence to indicate that this first IQ score is any more reliable or valid than subsequent scores. In speaking of this problem on the adult level, Bloom observes: "We find it hard to conceive of environments powerful enough to bring about an actual deterioration of adult intelligence. Such an environment would have to discourage and penalize the individual for utilizing the skills and problem solving abilities he had already developed" (1964, p. 85). It is generally acknowledged that early deprived and unfavorable environments in the preschool period slow up the development of potential, and that this loss of development in one period cannot be fully recovered in another period (Klineberg, 1957; Jersild, 1968; Hunt, 1961). However, such environmental stress would have diminished the Washington School scores on the very first intelligence test given, and barring a change in environment, no change in subsequent scores should have been expected (Stein and Susser, 1970).

If we use the IQ obtained in the first grade on the Pinter-Cunningham Primary Test of intelligence as a basic measure, we find that the so-called deterioration of IQ, if there is such a phenomenon, occurs substantially only among children in both schools who are above average in intelligence and seems unrelated to socioeconomic environment, as Table 4-2 shows.

Examination of the table indicates that large apparent losses in IQ were suffered only by children whose original scores were above 110. Such losses were as great in the Jefferson as in the Washington School. Losses among children with IQs below this were insignificant and well within the ±5 range of expectancy.

Similar results have been obtained in an unpublished study in which the New York City Board of Education's Bureau of Educational Research examined the IQ scores of children who were in a special program for the disadvantaged and of a control group. Here also children in low socioeconomic areas seemed to show no deterioration in IQ. Using the same tests as we used, with a population similar to our Washington School children, Harris and Lovinger (1968) compared IQ scores of 80 black students tested in the first, third, sixth, and eighth grades. They also concluded that there was no evidence of a declining IQ.

The whole question as to whether or not the numerical IQs changed over a period of years is perhaps of little importance. What is more important is whether the capacity to learn and the rate of learning changed. Aside from the IQ, there was no objective method of measuring these intangibles. Careful observations were therefore made by project staff and by teachers of those children who showed considerable deviations from one intelligence test to another. Although such observations were subjective, there was complete agreement that in no case did the pattern of learning or scores obtained on achievement tests parallel recorded changes in IQ. Whatever changes may have occurred were evidently related to factors other than intelligence.

A new policy of the New York City Board of Education eliminated the use of intelligence tests when our children were in senior high schools and forbade the recording of IQs on record cards. What, then, was the role and influence of IQs on the school progress of the children in the study? What action was taken by teachers and administrators as a result of the IQs obtained on intelligence tests in the first, third, sixth, and eighth grades? How did teachers use IQ scores?

Teachers' reliance on IQ scores and their concepts of the importance of these scores have been greatly exaggerated by the press, by some recent books on the evils of testing, and by well-meaning speakers who have had little contact with schools and with teachers. It will be recalled that one of the instruments used each year required teachers to identify each child's intellectual capacity as "exceptional," "average," "dull," "retarded." Even though IQ scores were available to teachers after the first

Table 4-2 Average Gain or Loss between Pintner-Cunningham and Other IQ Scores

| Range on Pintner-Cunningham Test | Otis Alpha | | | | Otis Beta | | Pintner Intermediate | | | |
|---|---|---|---|---|---|---|---|---|---|---|
| | N | | Gain or Loss | | Gain or Loss | | N | | Gain or Loss | |
| | Boys | Girls | Boys | Girls | Boys | Girls | Boys | Girls | Boys | Girls |
| | | | | | Jefferson School | | | | | |
| 130+ | 6 | 4 | −25.6 | −40.0 | −15.0 | −25.0 | 5 | 3 | −13.4 | −12.3 |
| 110–129 | 19 | 19 | −9.0 | −9.0 | −2.0 | −3.6 | 14 | 15 | 11.6 | −16.0 |
| 90–109 | 18 | 11 | −3.8 | −.3 | 9.6 | 3.7 | 10 | 11 | 9.4 | 22.0 |
| Below 90 | 3 | 4 | 4.3 | 1.0 | 2.7 | 3.8 | 3 | 3 | 6.3 | 11.3 |
| | | | | | Washington School | | | | | |
| 130+ | 1 | 0 | −14.0 | — | −35.0 | — | 1 | 0 | −28.0 | — |
| 110–129 | 9 | 9 | −15.0 | −11.6 | −18.0 | −8.3 | 7 | 5 | −13.6 | .4 |
| 90–109 | 14 | 28 | −4.0 | −.9 | .5 | 4.0 | 10 | 22 | −3.4 | 3.1 |
| Below 90 | 8 | 11 | 10.5 | 2.8 | 4.0 | −2.5 | 3 | 8 | −1.3 | −.1 |

year, it is noteworthy to observe how independent of these, teachers were in making judgments. It was not at all unusual for a teacher to say, "I know that Jane's IQ of 90 can't be accurate because she's functioning at a much higher level." And conversely, "Richard's IQ of 115 is far higher than his consistent performance would indicate. Could this be a valid score?"

This disregard for the recorded IQ score is best illustrated in the case of a child who was accelerated twice. In the first grade, he obtained an IQ of 119 on the Pintner-Cunningham Primary Test and in the third grade, 111 on the Otis Quick-Scoring Alpha Test. Nevertheless, teachers consistently rated him "exceptional" and treated him accordingly. Their concern and repeated requests for a more accurate IQ resulted in our arranging an individual intelligence examination for him where he obtained a Stanford-Binet IQ of 136. This intellectual superiority was again demonstrated in the junior high school where he obtained an IQ of 140 on the Pintner General Ability Intermediate Test.

Promotion and class placement, whether in homogeneous or heterogeneous grouping, were determined in both schools entirely on the basis of class performance and reading achievement test scores, and not IQ. It can be stated unequivocally that at no time during the elementary, junior, and senior high school years did an IQ score determine promotion or retention, or class placement or rejection, with the exception of a few children whose admission to the Special Progress program in the junior high schools was in question. Their problem and its resolution are discussed in the section on acceleration.

In the absence of IQ scores, how do teachers differentiate between their achievers and their underachievers? It is very difficult to see what other measure of potential would have been available to the teachers of our children, who were all sincere and consistent in their concern for underachievers.

There were, for example, a number of children whose scores on different intelligence tests varied so greatly, or whose IQs and performance were so disparate, that teachers asked for help in evaluating their children's potential. Arrangements were therefore made to have these children given individual intelligence examinations. As a result of such testing, teachers' suspicions and judgments were verified and several children in both schools were identified as serious underachievers. They were referred to remedial reading clinics, or they were assisted in obtaining private remedial instruction and/or therapy. It is possible that several among them would have been high school dropouts had teachers not been puzzled by inconsistencies between IQ scores and performance.

Our experience refutes the conclusions of Rosenthal and Jacobson (1968) that teachers' expectations become self-fulfilling prophecies. Had teachers been influenced by the IQ scores, their expectations would have led some children to better academic performance and hindered others from achievement that was noticeably superior.

Similar findings were obtained by Fleming and Anttonen (1971). In a study in which they gave teachers of 1087 children little or incorrect information about IQ scores, they conclude:

> It appears, that in the real world of the teacher using IQ test information, the self-fulfilling prophecy does not operate as Rosenthal hypothesizes. We can only conclude that teachers are more sensitive to the functioning level of students than previously believed. . . . [It] suggests that day to day living with the academic performance and behavior of children . . . provides more input than the results of an intelligence test administered on one given day [p. 250].

A previous effort by Clairborn (1969) to influence teacher expectancy also produced no change in teacher behavior or teacher-pupil interaction.

It must again be stated emphatically that during the entire course of this study, the only use that the IQ served was for the benefit of pupils. Our observations in other schools, with other principals and other teachers, indicates that this was generally the case.

### READING ACHIEVEMENT

It would be irrelevant to discuss here the complexity of the skills that are involved in the reading process. If there has not been an explosion in our knowledge of the subject, there has certainly been one in our interest and in our concern for more effective teaching in this area and much has been written on the subject.

It was neither intended nor possible to diagnose the causes of the difficulties which some of our children were encountering with reading. Nevertheless, their performance and achievement were of major importance to the study. In the elementary grades, promotion and retention were based almost entirely upon reading proficiency, a practice dictated by Board of Education directives. In the junior and senior high school grades, its relation to all other subjects was so great as to make reading virtually the determining factor in academic progress and in high school placement.

Attempts to measure growth in reading and to discern learning patterns emphasized the inadequacies of achievement tests as absolute measures but pointed up their value nevertheless as useful tools. Teacher judgment as a measure of progress, although very helpful, also presented difficulties. In some grades, teachers' judgments of competence in reading were clouded by strict adherence to the basal reader as a criterion of achievement. When teachers used such readers as the sole or major vehicle for their reading program, children's competence in reading was judged not by actual achievement, but within the limits of the reader that had been assigned. For example, teachers described children as reading "comfortably" and fluently on a third- or fourth-grade level, whereas such children might be reading just as "comfortably" and fluently on the next higher grade level, had they been given the reader of that level.

Standardized tests rather than teacher judgment were therefore used in measuring academic growth of pupils with the full realization of test inadequacies, of their limitations in measuring achievement among the very bright and the slow, and of some variability from one test to another. Moreover, our dependence on test scores was further justified by the fact that these scores were regularly added to the permanent record and were an important factor in the promotion and retention of children and in the admission of some children to Special Progress classes in the junior high schools.

The first standardized test given to the project children was the New York Reading Readiness Test, which was administered early in the first grade. As the name of the test indicates, it aims to measure readiness for formal reading instruction and gives scores in percentiles. Table 4-3 shows the distribution of scores obtained on this test. A few children were not available for testing.

The test manual states:

The percentile rating of 60 has been set as the minimum score at which children may be considered ready for reading instruction; with respect to the abilities being measured by the test—children obtaining a percentile score of 60 or above and who have adequate physical, social, and emotional maturity will probably be successful in learning to read at this time. Their rate of progress, however, will be influenced by such other factors as general intelligence, health, and attendance at school . . . [New York City Board of Education, 1947, p. 20].

If a percentile score of 60 is the cutoff point of "readiness," it would seem from Table 4-3 that approximately 80% of the boys and girls in the Jefferson School were "ready" for formal instruction and 62% of the boys and 55% of the girls in the Washington School were similarly "ready." This greater "readiness" of boys in the latter school was not borne out by subsequent achievement.

Table 4-3    New York Reading Readiness Test—Grade 1—Distribution of Scores

| Percentile | Jefferson School | | | Washington School | | |
|---|---|---|---|---|---|---|
| | Boys | Girls | Total | Boys | Girls | Total |
| 99 | | 1 | 1 | | | |
| 90 | 20 | 10 | 30 | 3 | 10 | 13 |
| 80 | 13 | 13 | 26 | 2 | 8 | 10 |
| 70 | 3 | 4 | 7 | 7 | 3 | 10 |
| 60 | 1 | 2 | 3 | 6 | 2 | 8 |
| 50 | 1 | 1 | 2 | 1 | 5 | 6 |
| 40 | 3 | 3 | 6 | 4 | 3 | 7 |
| 30 | 4 | | 4 | 1 | 1 | 2 |
| 20 | | | | 1 | 5 | 6 |
| 10 | 1 | 3 | 4 | 4 | 3 | 7 |
| 0 | | | | | 2 | 2 |
| Total $N$ | 46 | 37 | 83 | 29 | 42 | 71 |
| Median | 80 | 80 | 80 | 60 | 65 | 60 |

Since this test was given early in the school year and before formal reading instruction had begun, one may ponder over the variety of skills, potentials, and preparation for learning with which children enter our schools. The difference in median percentile scores between the two schools parallels the difference in mean IQs of the schools. Since the correlation between this reading readiness test and the Pintner-Cunningham Intelligence test was only .57 in the Jefferson School and .53 in the Washington School, factors in addition to intelligence must account for the difference in readiness and may very well account for differences in subsequent rates of learning. Coleman (1966), in a study of different ethnic populations, reported similar findings and noted that even in the first grade there are already large differences in the average level of achievement of different ethnic groups.

This difference in reading readiness between the two schools was followed by a similar difference in reading achievement, which was maintained more or less consistently throughout the grades. This consistency perhaps should have been expected. Bloom (1964) points out that by the time a child enters the first grade, 33% of his general achievement pattern has already been developed. Although the schools administered achievement tests in each grade, results of the citywide reading achievement tests given in the third, sixth, and ninth grades (Table 4-4) illustrate the increasing differences.

**Table 4-4  Metropolitan Achievement Tests—Reading**

| Test Level | | Jefferson School | | | Washington School | | |
|---|---|---|---|---|---|---|---|
| | | $N$ | Mean [a] | Standard Deviation | $N$ | Mean [a] | Standard Deviation |
| Elementary (Grade 3), Norm 3.4 | Boys | 46 | 4.0 | 1.04 | 32 | 3.3 | .91 |
| | Girls | 39 | 4.0 | .84 | 48 | 3.6 | .86 |
| | Total | 85 | 4.0 | .96 | 80 | 3.5 | .91 |
| Intermediate (Grade 6), Norm 5.9 | Boys | 43 | 7.5 | 2.02 | 32 | 5.8 | 2.05 |
| | Girls | 39 | 7.2 | 1.78 | 48 | 6.1 | 1.76 |
| | Total | 82 | 7.4 | 1.92 | 80 | 6.0 | 2.56 |
| Advanced (Grade 9), Norm 9.5 | Boys | 36 | 10.2 | 1.68 | 25 | 8.5 | 2.01 |
| | Girls | 36 | 9.9 | 1.84 | 40 | 9.0 | 2.04 |
| | Total | 72 | 10.1 | 1.77 | 65 | 8.8 | 2.09 |

[a] Mean grade equivalent.

Perhaps of greater interest and significance is the reading achievement level of the children during each of the elementary school grades. For this purpose, the grade norm has been interpreted to include a range of ±5 months. In too many cases, a difference of one correct, incorrect, or omitted item would have placed children above, at, or below the grade norm. This interpretation of the grade norm as a range is consistent with test manual data concerning the standard errors of the means.

The data given in Table 4-5 include the two citywide achievement tests previously described as well as the standardized reading achievement tests administered by the schools. This table seems to indicate that although boys started with approximately the same or higher median reading readiness percentile scores than did the girls in their schools, the divergencies that developed were in opposite directions in the two schools. In the Jefferson School, a larger percentage of boys than of girls read below the norm until the fourth grade when boys as a group surpassed the girls. In the Washington School, a larger percentage of boys than girls continued to read below the norm and a larger percentage of girls read above the norm in all grades. The national pattern of sex differences in the development of reading skills shows girls superior to boys at all ages and boys outnumbering girls in their need for corrective reading help (Dechant, 1970; Heilman, 1967). This is consistent with findings in the Washington School, but not in the Jefferson School where a larger percentage of boys than girls consistently achieved scores above the norm.

Let us again turn back to the interpretation of readiness percentile scores, quoted earlier from the test's *Manual of Directions*. How is a child's readiness to read as measured early in the first grade related to his reading achievement in the sixth and ninth grades? To what extent does the 60th percentile separate the potential achievers from the nonachievers, and thus predict performance? Table 4-6 presents group data from which partial answers may be obtained.

Although reading readiness is certainly related to reading achievement in the primary grades, its correlation with achievement test scores becomes lower in each succeeding grade and is never high enough to be used for prediction. The coefficients of correlation between scores on the New York Reading Readiness Test and scores on the Metropolitan Achievement Tests range from a high of .66 to a low of .38. A number of boys and girls in both schools who were below the 60th percentile managed to achieve at grade level, while some who were above this percentile did not maintain their level of performance.

More predictive of later achievement in reading was actual performance, even as early as the primary grades. The best readers in the

**Table 4-5** Reading Achievement Levels

| Grade | Norm (Grade Equivalent) | N | Below Norm N | Below Norm Percentage | Below Norm Range | At Norm N | At Norm Percentage | At Norm Range | Above Norm N | Above Norm Percentage | Above Norm Range |
|---|---|---|---|---|---|---|---|---|---|---|---|
| | | | | | Jefferson School | | | | | | |
| 2 | 1.9–2.9 | B, 46 | 5 | 10.9 | 1.7–1.8 | 9 | 19.6 | 1.9–2.9 | 32 | 69.5 | 3.1–3.8 |
| | | G, 38 | 1 | 2.6 | 1.7 | 11 | 28.9 | 1.9–2.9 | 26 | 68.5 | 3.1–3.8 |
| 3 | 2.9–3.9 | B, 46 | 8 | 17.4 | 1.5–2.7 | 13 | 28.3 | 2.9–3.9 | 25 | 54.3 | 4.1–5.6 |
| | | G, 39 | 4 | 10.3 | 2.2–2.7 | 14 | 35.9 | 3.0–3.9 | 21 | 53.8 | 4.2–5.4 |
| 4 | 3.9–4.9 | B, 46 | 8 | 17.4 | 2.8–3.7 | 9 | 19.6 | 3.9–4.9 | 29 | 63.0 | 5.0–8.5 |
| | | G, 39 | 8 | 20.5 | 3.0–3.8 | 10 | 25.6 | 4.0–4.8 | 21 | 53.9 | 5.1–7.5 |
| 5 | 4.6–5.6 | B, 46 | 6 | 13.0 | 3.3–4.3 | 6 | 13.0 | 4.9–5.5 | 34 | 74.0 | 5.7–10.7 |
| | | G, 39 | 7 | 17.9 | 3.1–4.5 | 9 | 23.1 | 4.6–5.6 | 23 | 59.0 | 5.7–9.1 |
| 6 | 5.4–6.4 | B, 43 | 5 | 11.6 | 3.5–4.8 | 5 | 11.6 | 5.4–6.4 | 33 | 76.8 | 6.5–11.6+ |
| | | G, 39 | 7 | 17.9 | 3.9–5.1 | 7 | 17.9 | 5.5–6.3 | 25 | 64.2 | 6.6–10.5 |
| 9[a] | 9.0–10.0 | B, 37 | 6 | 16.2 | 6.0–8.7 | 7 | 18.9 | 9.0–9.9 | 24 | 64.9 | 10.1–12.2 |
| | | G, 36 | 7 | 19.4 | 4.0–8.5 | 10 | 27.8 | 9.2–10.0 | 19 | 52.8 | 10.1–12.0 |
| | | | | | Washington School | | | | | | |
| 2 | 1.9–2.9 | B, 32 | 1 | 3.1 | 1.8 | 22 | 68.8 | 2.0–2.9 | 9 | 28.1 | 3.0–3.3 |
| | | G, 47 | 0 | — | 0 | 25 | 53.2 | 1.9–2.9 | 22 | 46.8 | 3.0–3.5 |
| 3 | 2.9–3.9 | B, 32 | 11 | 34.4 | 1.6–2.8 | 15 | 46.8 | 3.0–3.9 | 6 | 18.8 | 4.2–5.3 |
| | | G, 48 | 10 | 20.8 | 1.7–2.8 | 23 | 48.0 | 3.0–3.9 | 15 | 31.2 | 4.0–5.6 |
| 4 | 3.9–4.9 | B, 32 | 14 | 43.8 | 2.2–3.7 | 13 | 40.6 | 3.9–4.8 | 5 | 15.6 | 5.1–9.1 |
| | | G, 48 | 18 | 37.6 | 2.4–3.8 | 14 | 29.1 | 3.9–4.8 | 16 | 33.3 | 5.0–6.7 |
| 5 | 4.9–5.9 | B, 32 | 15 | 46.9 | 1.9–4.8 | 8 | 25.0 | 4.9–5.8 | 9 | 28.1 | 6.2–11.5 |
| | | G, 48 | 18 | 37.5 | 3.0–4.8 | 11 | 22.9 | 4.9–5.9 | 19 | 39.6 | 6.1–9.4 |
| 6 | 5.4–6.4 | B, 32 | 17 | 53.1 | 3.4–5.3 | 7 | 21.9 | 5.6–6.4 | 8 | 25.0 | 6.7–11.6 |
| | | G, 48 | 19 | 39.5 | 3.2–5.1 | 9 | 18.8 | 5.5–6.4 | 20 | 41.7 | 6.7–10.5 |
| 9[a] | 9.0–10.0 | B, 25 | 12 | 48.0 | 3.3–8.6 | 7 | 28.0 | 9.2–9.9 | 6 | 24.0 | 10.1–12.0 |
| | | G, 40 | 17 | 42.5 | 5.3–8.9 | 6 | 15.0 | 9.0–9.9 | 17 | 42.5 | 10.1–11.8 |

[a] Standardized reading achievement tests were not administered to all classes in the seventh and eighth grades.
B = Boys; G = Girls.

**Table 4-6  Relationship between Reading Readiness Percentile Scores and Sixth- and Ninth-Grade Reading Achievement Scores**

| First Grade | | Sixth Grade | | | | Ninth Grade | | | | | |
|---|---|---|---|---|---|---|---|---|---|---|---|
| Reading Readiness (Percentile) | Total $N^a$ | Achieved Grade Norm | | Did Not Achieve Grade Norm | | Total $N^a$ | Achieved Grade Norm | | Did Not Achieve Grade Norm | | |
| | | N | Percentage | N | Percentage | | N | Percentage | N | Percentage | |
| | | | | Jefferson School | | | | | | | |
| 60–99 | B, 35 | 33 | 94.3 | 2 | 5.7 | 29 | 26 | 89.7 | 3 | 10.3 | |
| | G, 30 | 29 | 96.7 | 1 | 3.3 | 28 | 26 | 92.9 | 2 | 7.1 | |
| 0–50 | B, 8 | 5 | 62.5 | 3 | 37.5 | 8 | 5 | 62.5 | 3 | 37.5 | |
| | G, 7 | 3 | 42.9 | 4 | 57.1 | 6 | 3 | 50.0 | 3 | 50.0 | |
| | | | | Washington School | | | | | | | |
| 60–99 | B, 18 | 11 | 61.1 | 7 | 38.9 | 14 | 8 | 57.1 | 6 | 42.9 | |
| | G, 23 | 19 | 82.6 | 4 | 17.4 | 20 | 15 | 75.0 | 5 | 25.0 | |
| 0–50 | B, 10 | 2 | 20.0 | 8 | 80.0 | 10 | 4 | 40.0 | 6 | 60.0 | |
| | G, 19 | 8 | 42.1 | 11 | 57.9 | 14 | 6 | 42.9 | 8 | 57.1 | |

[a] Missing scores and attrition account for variations in $N$.

B = Boys; G = Girls.

sixth and ninth grades of both schools were found among the best readers in the second grade and scored consistently above the grade norm; the poorest readers showed their difficulties just as early and for the most part continued to present reading problems.

It might be useful to summarize the relationships between early and subsequent standardized measures of reading performance. As mentioned previously, the tests that were administered were the New York Reading Readiness Test given in the first grade and the Metropolitan Reading Achievement Tests given in the third, sixth, and ninth grades.

Examination of the tables presented in this section and a close study of individual reading patterns among achieving and nonachieving children indicate that reading problems in the first and second grades must be viewed with anxiety but not with despair. Deep concern, however, and much thought must be given to children who, at the end of the third grade, are still presenting reading difficulties, for it is at this point that reading patterns seemed to become fairly well fixed. Figures in Table 4-7 show that the highest coefficients of correlation are found between third-grade reading achievement scores and subsequent test scores.

Table 4-7   Coefficients of Correlation between Reading Test Scores

|  | Jefferson School | | | Washington School | | |
|---|---|---|---|---|---|---|
|  | Boys | Girls | Total | Boys | Girls | Total |
| Reading Readiness and Third Grade | .55 | .65 | .58 | .61 | .50 | .55 |
| Reading Readiness and Sixth Grade | .47 | .66 | .56 | .50 | .48 | .49 |
| Reading Readiness and Ninth Grade | .45 | .63 | .56 | .57 | .38 | .47 |
| Third Grade and Sixth Grade | .79 | .86 | .80 | .81 | .80 | .80 |
| Third Grade and Ninth Grade | .73 | .81 | .75 | .73 | .76 | .74 |

The significance of third-grade reading achievement scores is heightened if we examine Tables A-1 to A-4 in the Appendix, which show correlations between all citywide, standardized intelligence and achievement tests administered to our childern from Grades 1 through 9. These tests were accepted by the schools as important measures of potential and achievement.

It will be seen from these tables that the earliest measure showing a high and consistent correlation with subsequent intelligence tests and with achievement tests, both in reading and mathematics, is the third-grade reading achievement test. This was characteristic of both schools, and in every case, coefficients of correlation with the five subsequent tests were greater than with any of the three previous tests.

It may be that, beginning in the middle grades, tests become weighted in favor of those having verbal skills. Nevertheless, general academic performance also seems to be based on verbal ability and, as a result, third-grade reading scores could have been used for most of our children as predictors of success or failure certainly during the following six years, the high school years, and even well beyond.

How, then, can early patterns of failure be changed? How are teachers being helped to meet reading problems? On the basis of observations made in many classrooms both in project schools and in other schools, one must conclude that our expectations of teachers in elementary, self-contained classrooms are somewhat unrealistic. Teachers are expected to be competent, if not expert, in teaching all curriculum areas including reading. In this area they are asked not only to provide instruction but also to diagnose the reading difficulties that children present and to provide remedial drill as needed.

This is a task which even psychologists and clinical personnel find formidable. It is a fallacious assumption that complex reading problems can be broken down into simple, identifiable elements which teachers can easily recognize, and for each of which there are specific remedial drills. Teachers are provided with checklists or with cards which purport to tabulate or to describe in sequential order the development of skills necessary for success in reading. But the teacher's problem in pinpointing the specific skills in which any single child is deficient remains unsolved. Moreover, the additional time and attention that deficient readers require is usually ignored in fixing class registers; and more often than not, teachers are supplied with the same readers and reading materials with which their children had originally met failure.

The frequently repeated charge that poor teaching is the major cause of reading deficiency is an oversimplification of a difficult problem. Even our most able teachers were unable to help some of our children. The only early reading failures who were able to break the pattern were the few who could be accommodated at special reading clinics or who received intensive help from an available remedial reading specialist, or whose parents were able to secure private therapy and/or remedial assistance. For example:

Steven, with a Stanford-Binet IQ of 100, ranked in the 40th percentile on the New York Reading Readiness Test given early in the first grade. He made very slight progress in reading in the first grade and at the end of the second grade he was classified as a retarded reader. In the third grade Steven was placed in a specially organized class having a small register and consisting of the poorest readers in the grade. Although the teacher had been carefully selected and was very skillful, Steven made little progress, and at the end of the third grade, he was two years retarded in reading.

The school referred him to a child guidance clinic and while waiting to be called, his mother secured the services of a private tutor. Private lessons along with therapy at the clinic were continued from the fourth through the seventh grade. This special help in a one-to-one relationship with the tutor and the therapist was very effective, and by the ninth grade, Steven was reading and functioning above grade level.

He received satisfactory grades both in high school and in junior college where he studied Hotel Management, a field in which he is now successfully employed.

Another such child was Henry:

Henry's facility with language and his excellent vocabulary were apparent from the time he entered kindergarten. His reading readiness rating in the first grade placed him in the 90th percentile and he obtained an IQ of 107 on the Pintner-Cunningham Test. Nevertheless, he seemed to have much difficulty with reading. He was retarded in reading in grades one and two, and in the third grade he was placed in a class which was especially organized for slow readers. This did not seem to help Henry and his parents became understandably concerned over his reading deficiency. At the end of the third grade, they agreed to have him referred to a child guidance clinic and early the next year when he was given a Stanford-Binet Test, he obtained an IQ of 121. His mother was seen regularly by a social worker and provision was made by the principal of his school to have Henry attend an after-school reading clinic in the community twice weekly.

Henry, who always showed a need for adult approval, seemed very pleased with this special attention and went for the instruction eagerly. He once said, "I'm glad I'm going. I need help, the faster the better." Whenever he worked on an assignment he needed assurance and approval and he would frequently go to his teacher to ask, "Isn't this good?" By the time he reached the fifth grade, he was making slow progress, but from then on he made greater and greater strides. He especially enjoyed the opportunities he was given to read to the principal, to the Project Assistant, and to his teacher to show the progress he was making. By the end of Grade 6 he was reading above his grade level and continued to do well in junior and senior high school.

Efforts in providing schools with remedial reading personnel and in decreasing class size are all to the good. Major responsibility for helping children who present reading problems has to be assumed by specially trained personnel working with classroom teachers, as these two cases indicate.

# CHAPTER FIVE

## Children Who Differed

### THE FAILURES

When our children were in the primary grades, the school system abandoned its continuous progress promotion policy, which had been in effect for more than a decade, and returned to the practice of holding children back to repeat a grade when their reading achievement was not considered satisfactory.

Whatever the reasons were for the change in promotion policy, they were not based upon the findings of research. The Board of Education's own Director of Research wrote:

Research on nonpromotion over the past 40 years has shown that it is generally ineffective. The findings from numerous studies are:

Children at any ability level do not learn more by repeating a grade. Actually, most of them make less progress in learning subject-matter than if they are promoted to the next grade. For instance, a study of children with low IQ's who had repeated several grades revealed that they were not doing as well in their schoolwork as children of similar ability who had been kept with those of approximately their own age.

Nonpromotion affects the personality of the pupil unfavorably. Clinical studies of children who have failed show that there is a loss of self-confidence. Self-respect is undermined. The feeling of security, so necessary to mental health, is usually weakened and feelings of inferiority are increased [Wright-stone, 1957, pp. 4–5].

Studies and observations prior and subsequent to Wrightstone's publication consistently uphold his summary.

According to a study by Caswell (1933), nonpromotion does not assure mastery of subject matter or lead to greater homogeneity of mental ability. Nonpromotion does increase disciplinary problems and intensify emotional instability. Caswell found that retaining a child may kill his incentive, lower his achievement, and produce undesirable effects on his personality.

Sandin (1944) reported that children in the upper elementary grades who are not promoted tend to be isolates in the new class. The children select companions from the grade above theirs and develop attitudes toward school that become increasingly negative.

According to Goodlad (1952), first and second graders who had not been promoted also showed a tendency toward isolation, though for the children in the lower grades the tendency was less marked than for the children in the upper elementary grades.

A survey led Mallinson and Weston (1954) to conclude that nonpromotion is ineffective in dealing with the problem of slow learners. Nonpromoted children achieved less than they would have had they been promoted. Motivation suffered, and maladjustment was more common after nonpromotion than before. The authors recommended that the teacher who is considering nonpromotion study a broad array of facts to learn why the child is not doing well in school. Insight into that question may help the teacher arrive at a sound decision as to whether nonpromotion will help the pupil overcome his difficulties.

In 1948, a questionnaire study of 93 school systems brought together the pros and cons of a nonfailure policy (National Education Association, 1950). In support of the policy, it was pointed out that keeping a child with his own age group made for the soundest emotional, mental, physical, and social growth and adjustment. The policy reduced behavior problems, helped develop good work habits, and gave the child an opportunity to work according to his ability. In addition, the teachers found more satisfaction in the policy of no failures, for under the old promotion plan, the teacher had to press the child to try to do what he really could not do.

Respondents who argued against the policy pointed out that it reduced incentive for superior scholastic achievement. It led to problems for children who found the work beyond their capacity. It created problems for the teacher who had to work with classes that had a wide range in achievement. It caused problems for parents; it created problems in high school; it produced administrative problems.

Steadman (1959) reports a study of the records of 15 children who had been retained in a grade. Written evaluations by teachers and data from record cards at the time of retention were submitted to eight judges who were asked whether each child should have been retained. Only for seven children was there agreement by more than half the judges, and all the judges were in agreement on only one of these children.

Some evidence of the effect of retention upon children is revealed by three questions that were asked of them when they had reached the seventh and eighth grades:

1. Do you feel that it was a good idea to retain you?
2. How has retention helped you?
3. How has retention hurt you?

A boy retained in the first grade said, "It was too soon to tell how a person will work in studies. It took me a long time to adjust to it. You don't care for a while. I felt so much more inferior, yet bigger and older. When I did adjust, the first thing I wanted to do was to get ahead a grade." Another boy commented, "I was pretty unhappy for three or four years."

Steadman concludes: "At the very least, the children's responses should make us cautious in forming decisions that can have such a far-reaching effect on a child's life" (pp. 275–276).

In summarizing research findings on the subject of promotion, Otto and Estes conclude as follows:

For one, each child seems to grow and develop in accordance with his own individual growth pattern; his growth in achievement is closely associated with this pattern; and the rate at which different children grow and develop ranges from very slow to very rapid, with most children clustering around a midpoint between these two extremes. If absurd extremes are avoided, exact grade placement has little or no bearing upon the educational development a child will make during a given year. Repetition of grades has no special educational value for children; in fact, the educational gain of the majority of nonpromoted students subsequent to their nonpromotion is smaller than that of their matched agemates who were promoted. Similarly, the threat of failure has no appreciable positive effect on the educational gain of those threatened. The personal and social adjustment of regularly promoted students is better than that of students who have experienced nonpromotion, and the average level of student achievement tends to be higher in school systems with high promotion rates [1960, p. 8].

Later research completely supports these findings. Kowitz and Armstrong (1961) conclude that, "Evidence is lacking that retention increases the pupil's academic proficiency" (p. 435) and "those who had not made normal progress continued to form a separate group that showed less achievement even after retention, [suggesting] that their extra year had not eliminated the difference in their achievement" (p. 437).

More recent observations on nonpromotion repeat the warnings. Johnson and Medinnus (1969) speak of the effect of repeated failures on the child's self-esteem, and Glasser states that, "Once a child receives the failure label and sees himself as a failure, he will rarely succeed in school" (1969, p. 97). Strom comments, "The practice of nonpromotion as a response to failure remains an obstacle to achievement" (1969, p. 66), and he describes studies showing the high correlation between non-promotion in the elementary grades and subsequent "dropping out" in high school.

Returning now to our two schools, it is difficult at this writing to see what motivated the Board of Education. In spite of all the research on the subject, and the opposition of some of the professional staff, the new policy of nonpromotion was officially announced and a directive was sent to all elementary schools setting up guidelines for teachers and principals.

The directions given annually, with slight variations in wording, are as follows (New York City Board of Education, 1955–1956 *et seq.*):

We believe that reading has such high correlation with ability in other curriculum areas that it may be used as a major factor in grading and classification.

Children who fall far behind their grade benefit from retention in the grade . . . . Retention in Grades 1–6 is not to occur more than once.

At the end of the second grade, children who are still at the reading readiness level should be retained.

Children in the third grade who have fallen two years below grade in reading but who have not been retained, may be retained by placement in a regular class in Grade 3 with special help in reading or in an Opportunity Class in Grade 3.

Children who have not been retained in the lower grades may be retained in Grades 4–6.

Children with reading grades below 5.0 who have not been retained once in Grades K–6 must not be sent on to junior high school, unless in cases where the approval of the assistant superintendent has been secured.

These guidelines were interpreted in many schools as referring to the annual reading achievement test results, which were then used for determining grade placement. Gerberich and Blaha caution against this practice and state, "strong reliance on test results in making decisions about the promotion of pupils on a regular basis, or about their retardation or acceleration would be dangerous" (1961, p. 21). Ginsburg decries this preoccupation with tests and comments, "One of the faulty assumptions underlying the traditional school is that standard tests measure important aspects of knowledge. . . . On the contrary, in many cases standard tests and classroom examinations fail to capture much that is important about children's cognition" (1972, pp. 200–201).

Nevertheless, the extent of literal adherence to these suggestions and to holdover policy seemed to differ somewhat from school to school. The final decision as to whether a child was to be retained in a grade rested with the principal, and in some cases with the field superintendent.

Throughout the course of this study, there were no basic children held back in the Jefferson School but a few children of the next higher class were left back into the grade then under study. This, however, was not the case in the Washington School, where both situations occurred. This presented an unusual opportunity to study the effects of retention on a group of children for whom so much data were available.

No basic children in the Washington School were held back before the fifth grade. At the end of the fifth grade, four boys and four girls were retained in the grade. Nevertheless, an attempt was made to continue contact with them and toward the end of their second year in the fifth grade, teachers of these eight children were asked to provide data on the same scales that had previously been used. Table 5-1 indicates IQs, scores, and ratings obtained at the end of the first year that these children spent in the fifth grade and again at the end of the second year in the same grade.

Examination of the data in Table 5-1 indicates that the additional year spent in the fifth grade resulted in an aggregate gain of one year and two months and an aggregate loss of two years as measured by achievement in reading. If we compare the loss or gain in reading for each child during the year of retention with the average gain made during the years in which no retention occurred, we note that in no case did repeating a grade result in progress even equal to the average gain shown during the years of promotion. One must conclude that, for these children, retention had a deleterious effect upon progress in reading. It is ironical that the very purposes which retention in the grade was supposed to have served were so completely unrealized.

Furthermore, three of the eight children indicate a deteriorating attitude toward classroom activity and, by inference, toward school. Four show no change at all, and only one shows an improvement in attitude.

**Table 5-1** Nonpromoted Grade 5 Pupils—Scores and Ratings before and after Repeating Fifth Grade [a] Washington School

| Pupil | IQ Test | IQ Score | Reading Scores 5¹ | Reading Scores 5² | Gain or Loss | Prom. Aver. Gain | Attitude to Classroom Activity 5¹ | Attitude to Classroom Activity 5² | General Adjustment 5¹ | General Adjustment 5² | Listed as Adjustment Problem 5¹ | Listed as Adjustment Problem 5² | Also Listed as Problem in Grade |
|---|---|---|---|---|---|---|---|---|---|---|---|---|---|
| Alfred | K.A. | 73 | 3.2 | 3.3 | .1 | .6 | I | P | 1 | 2 | — | — | — |
| Benjamin | P.C. | 74 | 3.0 | 2.5 | -.5 | .6 | P | I | 4 | 1 | — | — | — |
|  | Otis A | 75 |  |  |  |  |  |  |  |  |  |  |  |
| Andrew | P.C. | 95 | 3.1 | 3.3 | .2 | .6 | I | I | 3 | 3 | — | x | 4 |
|  | Otis A | 86 |  |  |  |  |  |  |  |  |  |  |  |
| Joseph | P.C. | 84 | 3.3 | 2.5 | -.8 | .5 | P | P | 3 | 4 | — | x | — |
|  | Otis A | 84 |  |  |  |  |  |  |  |  |  |  |  |
| Jessica | P.C. | 94 | 3.5 | 4.0 | .5 | .7 | I | I | 2 | 1 | — | — | — |
|  | Otis A | 76 |  |  |  |  |  |  |  |  |  |  |  |
| Nancy | P.C. | 80 | 3.3 | 3.6 | .3 | .7 | E | P | 3 | 3 | — | x | — |
|  | Otis A | 96 |  |  |  |  |  |  |  |  |  |  |  |
| Pauline | P.C. | 75 | 3.0 | 3.1 | .1 | .6 | I | U | 5 | 4 | x | x | 4 |
|  | Otis A | 69 |  |  |  |  |  |  |  |  |  |  |  |
| Gladys | Not tested—language difficulty |  | 3.2 | 2.5 | -.7 | .5 | I | I | 1 | 1 | — | — | — |

[a] The following abbreviations are used: K.A. = Kuhlman Anderson Intelligence Tests; P.C. = Pintner-Cunningham Primary Test; Otis A = Otis Quick-Scoring Mental Ability Tests, Alpha; Otis B = Otis Quick-Scoring Mental Ability Tests, Beta; 5¹ = first fifth-grade experience; 5² = second fifth-grade experience; Prom. Aver. Gain = average gain in reading made during years of promotion. Attitude to Classroom Activity is rated as follows: E = enthusiastic; I = interested; P = passive; U = uninterested. General Adjustment is rated on a scale of 1, very well adjusted, to 5, very poorly adjusted.

Table 5-2  Nonpromoted Grade 6 Pupils—Scores and Ratings before and after Repeating Sixth Grade [a] Washington School

| Pupil | IQ Test | IQ Score | Reading Scores 6¹ | Reading Scores 6² | Gain or Loss | Prom. Aver. Gain | Attitude to Classroom Activity 6¹ | Attitude to Classroom Activity 6² | General Adjustment 6¹ | General Adjustment 6² | Listed as Adjustment Problem 6¹ | Listed as Adjustment Problem 6² | Also Listed as Problem in Grade |
|---|---|---|---|---|---|---|---|---|---|---|---|---|---|
| Carl | P.C. | 96 | 4.3 | 5.1 | .8 | .7 | U | P | 5 | 4 | x | x | 3 |
|  | K.A. | 86 | | | | | | | | | | | |
|  | Otis B | 78 | | | | | | | | | | | |
| Daniel | P.C. | 85 | 2.2 | 3.0 | .8 | .4 | P | P | 4 | 3 | x | x | — |
|  | Otis A | 92 | | | | | | | | | | | |
|  | Otis B | 71 | | | | | | | | | | | |
| Doris | P.C. | 66 | 3.2 | 3.7 | .5 | .5 | P | P | 3 | 4 | — | — | 1 |
|  | Otis A | 84 | | | | | | | | | | | |
|  | Otis B | 82 | | | | | | | | | | | |
| Helen | K.A. | 104 | 3.5 | 3.7 | .2 | .6 | I | I | 2 | 2 | — | — | — |
|  | Otis A | 88 | | | | | | | | | | | |
|  | Otis B | 76 | | | | | | | | | | | |
| May | Otis A | 76 | 4.6 | 3.4 | -1.2 | .8 | I | I | 2 | 2 | — | — | — |
| Lois | Otis A | 81 | 3.7 | 4.4 | .7 | .6 | P | I | 4 | 3 | — | x | — |
|  | Otis B | 79 | | | | | | | | | | | |

[a] See Table 5-1 for key.

This one, Benjamin, also shows a great improvement in his general adjustment. Along with this improvement, however, went a five-month loss in reading ability as measured by the achievement tests. Ratings in general adjustment at the end of each of the years are inconclusive. Most striking, however, is the fact that at the end of the first year in the fifth grade only one of the eight children had been reported as exhibiting problems of behavior and adjustment, whereas at the end of the second year in the fifth grade, four of these eight were so reported. Of these four, only two had been reported previously as adjustment problems. Glasser (1971) indicates that this is a common occurrence and that when children are labeled as failures, they begin to behave like failures. The ego-deflating effects of failure and its negative impact upon behavior appear consistently in studies and discussions of retention (Farley et al., 1933; McElvee, 1936; Anfinson, 1941; Sandin, 1944; Hurlock, 1972).

Although not part of our basic population, other children who had been held back at various times crossed our path and supplied interesting data which warranted examination. One such group consisted of those who were retained in the sixth grade and for whom data identical to those given in Table 5-1 were available, as shown in Table 5-2.

Here again, the average gain of three months made by these children during their year of retention was half the average gain in reading that they had made during their years of promotion, although three children do show individual gains. As can be seen, changes in attitude and general adjustment were minor, and Lois, who had never before been identified as an adjustment problem, was now so listed after repeating the sixth grade.

Another group that was held over consisted of those children who had been held back in the third, fourth, fifth, or sixth grades and thus found themselves at various times in classes with the children then being studied. Table 5-3 indicates first and second scores in reading in the grade repeated, the gain or loss, the average gain for each child during the years in which he was promoted, and the reading scores in each of the other grades. The IQs listed are those obtained on the Otis Quick-Scoring Mental Ability Tests—Alpha.

Of the 33 pupils who were held back and who were officially labeled "failure," only two gained more than a year when they were held over in the grade. Another seven made slight gains over their average growth during their years of promotion, but these were in terms of one or a few months, differences that were insignificant. The other 24 either showed no gain or recorded losses. Identical results were obtained in a study by Saunders, who writes, "From the evidence cited, it may be concluded

Table 5-3  Pupil Retention—Reading Progress during Promotion
and Retention—Washington School

| Grade Repeated | Otis Alpha IQ | Reading Score 1st | Reading Score 2nd | Gain or Loss | Prom. [a] Aver. Gain | Reading Scores [c] Grade 2 | 3 | 4 | 5 | 6 |
|---|---|---|---|---|---|---|---|---|---|---|
| **Grade 6** | | | | | | | | | | |
| Carl | 81 | 4.3 | 5.1 | .8 | .7 | 2.0 | 2.4 | 3.3 | 4.0 | [b] |
| Daniel | 92 | 2.2 | 3.0 | .8 | .4 | 1.8 | 1.7 | 2.6 | 3.3 | [b] |
| Dot | 84 | 3.2 | 3.7 | .5 | .5 | 1.9 | 1.9 | 2.6 | 3.5 | [b] |
| Gary | 82 | 3.4 | 4.1 | .7 | .6 | — | 1.7 | 2.5 | 2.9 | [b] |
| Grace | 89 | 4.2 | 4.7 | .5 | .7 | 2.5 | 3.1 | 3.0 | 3.8 | [b] |
| Hannah | 70 | 3.5 | 3.8 | .3 | .6 | 1.8 | 1.3 | — | — | [b] |
| Helen | 88 | 3.5 | 3.7 | .2 | .6 | — | 1.6 | 2.8 | — | [b] |
| Jane | 81 | 3.5 | 4.3 | .8 | .6 | 1.4 | 2.4 | 3.2 | 4.7 | [b] |
| Lee | 92 | 3.4 | 4.0 | .6 | .6 | 2.4 | 2.5 | 3.3 | 3.8 | [b] |
| Lola | 81 | 4.6 | 5.2 | .6 | .6 | — | 1.9 | — | 3.5 | [b] |
| May | 100 | 3.8 | 4.2 | .4 | .6 | 1.8 | 1.2 | 3.3 | 3.8 | [b] |
| Ray | 76 | 4.6 | 3.4 | −1.2 | .8 | — | 2.2 | 2.5 | 3.4 | [b] |
| Sue | 69 | 3.3 | 3.9 | .6 | .6 | 1.8 | 1.7 | — | — | [b] |
| Victor | 105 | 3.9 | 3.8 | −.1 | .7 | 2.0 | 1.8 | 2.4 | — | [b] |
| **Grade 5** | | | | | | | | | | |
| Andy | 73 | 3.2 | 3.3 | .1 | .6 | — | 2.1 | 2.2 | [b] | 4.1 |
| Bob | 75 | 3.0 | 2.5 | −.5 | .6 | 2.0 | 2.2 | 2.0 | [b] | 3.4 |
| Cal | 95 | 4.4 | 4.9 | .5 | .9 | 2.6 | 2.2 | 3.1 | [b] | 4.9 |
| Gay | — | 3.2 | 2.5 | −.7 | .5 | — | — | 2.2 | [b] | — |
| Gert | 112 | 2.9 | 4.0 | 1.1 | .6 | 2.3 | — | 2.9 | [b] | 3.8 |
| Joan | 76 | 3.5 | 4.0 | .5 | .7 | 2.1 | 2.3 | 3.0 | [b] | — |
| John | 84 | 3.3 | 2.5 | −.8 | .5 | 2.5 | 2.3 | 2.0 | [b] | 3.1 |
| Mat | 86 | 3.1 | 3.3 | .2 | .6 | 1.8 | 2.1 | 2.3 | [b] | — |
| Mel | 85 | 3.2 | 3.8 | .6 | .6 | 2.5 | 2.5 | 1.8 | [b] | 3.9 |
| Nell | 96 | 3.3 | 3.6 | .3 | .7 | 2.3 | 2.2 | 1.8 | [b] | — |
| Pam | 80 | 3.5 | 3.8 | .3 | .7 | 1.8 | 1.8 | 2.4 | [b] | 4.5 |
| Pat | 69 | 3.0 | 3.1 | .1 | .6 | 2.6 | 2.3 | 3.1 | [b] | 3.9 |
| **Grade 4** | | | | | | | | | | |
| Bess | 97 | 2.1 | 3.0 | .9 | .5 | — | 1.6 | [b] | 3.6 | 3.8 |
| **Grade 3** | | | | | | | | | | |
| Dan | 89 | 1.7 | 2.1 | .4 | .5 | 1.9 | [b] | — | — | — |
| Ford | 93 | 1.9 | 3.0 | 1.1 | .6 | 2.4 | [b] | 3.7 | 4.2 | 5.0 |
| Fred | 95 | 1.4 | 1.7 | .3 | .5 | — | [b] | 2.7 | 3.4 | 3.4 |

Table 5-3    Pupil Retention—Reading Progress during Promotion
and Retention—Washington School (Cont.)

| Grade Repeated | Otis Alpha IQ | Reading Score | | Gain or Loss | Prom.[a] Aver. Gain | Reading Scores [c] Grade | | | | |
|---|---|---|---|---|---|---|---|---|---|---|
| | | 1st | 2nd | | | 2 | 3 | 4 | 5 | 6 |
| Jack | 92 | 2.0 | 2.8 | .8 | .7 | 2.3 | [b] | 3.4 | 4.3 | — |
| Jill | 102 | 2.2 | 2.9 | .7 | .7 | 2.9 | [b] | 3.2 | 4.5 | 4.9 |
| Will | 77 | 1.3 | 2.2 | .9 | .4 | 1.7 | [b] | 3.1 | 4.0 | — |

[a] Average gain made during years of promotion.
[b] Grade repeated; first and second reading scores shown in columns 3 and 4 under Reading Score.
[c] Grade equivalent.

that nonpromotion of pupils in elementary schools in order to assure mastery of subject matter does not often accomplish its objectives. Children do not appear to learn more by repeating a grade but experience less growth in subject matter achievement than they do when promoted" (1941, p. 29). Similar conclusions were drawn by Coffield and Blommers (1956) and by Dobbs and Neville (1967).

Almost all of these pupils had been given various forms of the Metropolitan Reading Tests, and also several levels of the test. In the first two grades and sometimes beyond that, the Primary level was used extensively. In subsequent grades the level considered most appropriate was given. In the absence of pathology, we cannot say that pupils sustained losses in their reading skills. Such losses and even gains may be a function of the different test levels used rather than of actual loss or progress, or they may be a result of physical or emotional factors involved in pupil test responses. Examination of the scoring directions in the Primary, Elementary, and Intermediate levels of the Metropolitan Reading Tests indicates overlapping and areas where growth as measured on two levels cannot always be accurately determined.

It may be that scores achieved at the end of the first year in the grade were reasonable expectations for our children entirely consistent with IQ and other intangible factors involved in learning (Rohwer, 1971), and that whatever gains seem to have been made subsequently might also have been made had these children not been held over. If we observe the traumatic effects which being held back have upon some children and their families, one must conclude that the value of such practices needs constant reexamination, and its use in determining grade placement requires greater understanding and wisdom. Abidin, Golladay, and Howerton suggest "that when educators retain a child they frequently doom his educational career and, in the case of the poverty child, they could thus possibly ruin his one major opportunity to change his life circumstances" (1971, p. 415).

Perhaps we should first reexamine the rationale—"the philosophy, inherent in much of our education, that if you fail a child it will cause him to buckle down and work hard; it will make a new man of him. Unfortunately, it just doesn't work that way. Most of us by this time know that all you learn from failing is how to fail. And in our schools we are teaching many, many children how to fail" (Glasser, 1971, p. 6).

## THE ACCELERATED

Although New York City never officially adopted a three-track plan of progress, in practice, it did exist. Data have already been presented for those children who completed the first six grades in six years and who continued to make normal progress throughout their schooling. The preceding section was concerned with those children who took a longer time to complete their elementary school education. We turn now to those children who were chosen to accelerate their progress through the elementary and junior high school years, and who entered college and their careers at an earlier age.

There were two ways in which progress through New York City schools could be accelerated. One was by completing either the first three grades, or the fourth, fifth, and sixth in two years. Bright children were sometimes permitted to do this, but only three of our children were accelerated in this way. The other and more common way was by admission to the Special Progress (SP) classes in the junior high school following the completion of the sixth grade of elementary school. There were, at the time, two types of SP class in the New York City junior high schools. In one, children completed the three-year course in two years, not by skipping but by telescoping and accelerating the three-year program. The other type of SP class involved no acceleration but presented the three-year program with intensive enrichment in the various subjects over a three-year period. Although transfer from the two-year program to the three-year progam was permitted, the reverse was not. This program is still in effect.

Requirements for admission to both types of class were identical, but the decision as to whether a child would enter a two-year or a three-year program generally was left to parents. Requirements for admission to the SP classes were given in annual directives from the Superintendent of Schools as follows:

Pupils selected for these classes must possess ALL of the following qualifications:

1. Personal characteristics of initiative, enthusiasm, willingness to work, reliability, industry, regular attendance, and capacity for sustained work.

2. For the two-year course, pupils must have the social maturity on a level with the average thirteen year old.

3. Good physical health; no evidence of emotional instability.

4. An IQ of 125 obtained on an individual psychological examination under the auspices of the Board of Education or an average IQ of 125 obtained on two group intelligence tests within the past three years.

5. A reading level of 8.0 on a standardized reading test at the time the test is administered.

6. An arithmetic level of 8.0 on a standardized test at the time the test is administered.

7. For the two-year course, a minimum chronological age of 11 years, 3 months at the time of admission.

These requirements were preceded in the official directive with a statement, "It is the responsibility of both the principal of the elementary school and the principal of the junior high school to make certain that there is strict conformity with the standards for admission of pupils to the special progress classes." The directive continues with the admonition, "Principals of elementary schools with sixth-year classes will select the children eligible for SP classes in accordance with the above requirements. *There must be no exceptions as to the requirements.*"

If these requirements for admission seem rigid, it should be pointed out that there was considerable justification for rigidity. In a school system where 73,000 children complete the sixth grade each year, such requirements may be necessary in order to achieve some conformity and some uniformity in the caliber of SP classes. Any other method might leave the decision to individual teachers in all parts of the city, and might create SP classes which differ widely from each other. Current admission requirements are far less stringent and omit IQ as a criterion.

In the Jefferson School 18 boys and 11 girls met the requirements for admission, and in the Washington School three boys were eligible. There were, however, other boys and girls in both schools who could not meet the minimum qualifications in all categories but who were considered by their teachers to have the potentials for success in the SP program. In the Jefferson School five boys and three girls, and in the

Table 5-4 Data for Achievers Lacking Minimum IQ for SP Program—Jefferson School

| | Elementary School | | | | | | Junior High School | | |
| | IQ | | | | Grade Score | | | Grade Score | |
| | Pintner-Cunningham | Otis Alpha | Otis Beta | Hennon-Nelson | Metropolitan Intermediate Reading | Metropolitan Intermediate Mathematics | Pintner Intermediate IQ | Metropolitan Advanced Reading | Average—Major Subjects (%) |
| Grade: | 1 | 3 | 6 | 6 | 6 | 6 | 9 | 9 | 7-9 |
|---|---|---|---|---|---|---|---|---|---|
| Boys | | | | | | | | | |
| R.M. | 94 | 101 | 115 | 125 | 9.0 | 9.5 | 136 | 11.0 | 88.6 |
| S.R. | 126 | 102 | 122 | 132 | 9.8 | 10.0 | 131 | 11.4 | 92.8 |
| A.A. | 141 | 101 | 117 | 139 | 8.5 | 10.1 | 136 | 11.2 | 97.0 [a] |
| B.R. | 112 | 110 | 123 | 125 | 9.9 | 9.0 | 137 | 12.1 | 72.6 |
| C.K. | 113 | 108 | 118 | 125 | 9.6 | 9.2 | 129 | 10.1 | 75.0 |
| Girls | | | | | | | | | |
| C.B. | 125 | 132 | 124 | 125 | 10.3 | 8.0 | 125 | 10.6 | 89.8 |
| G.M. | 115 | 131 | 123 | 141 | 8.7 | 9.6 | 148 | 12.0 | 92.8 |
| G.I. | 107 | 91 | 118 | 125 | 10.3 | 8.0 | 117 | 11.6 | 86.8 |

[a] Valedictorian at graduation from junior high school and again from senior high school.

Washington School one boy and seven girls met the requirements in all categories except that of IQ.

After considerable discussion and a reassessment of the achievement of these children over a six-year period, it was felt in both schools that their demonstrated performance had higher validity than the IQ obtained on the Otis Beta Test, or even those obtained earlier. The schools therefore administered the Henmon-Nelson Test of Mental Ability to these 16 children, and their IQ scores now ranged from 125 to 141. As a result, all of them were declared eligible for the SP classes.

Data concerning their subsequent junior high school scores as well as their previous scores in intelligence and achievement are given in Table 5-4. In all but one case, teachers' judgments were vindicated and their confidence in the children was justified.

These eight children had scores on the Metropolitan Intermediate Reading Test, given in the sixth grade, ranging from 8.5 to 10.3 and on the Metropolitan Intermediate Mathematics Test, also given in the sixth grade, from 8.0 to 10.1. None of these children, however, had obtained IQs of 125 or higher on the Otis Beta Test and since no other intelligence test had been administered during the previous three years, these eight children were definitely ineligible.

In the Advanced Metropolitan Reading Test given in the ninth grade, the scores of these eight children ranged from 10.1 to 12.1 with a mean of 11.3. Furthermore, in the same year the Pintner General Ability Intermediate Test was administered to these children and they now obtained IQ scores which ranged from 117 to 148, only one girl scoring below 125. In examining their general performance and achievement in the junior high schools one notes that almost all of these children, who ordinarily would not have been admitted to the SP classes, achieved well above the mean for these special classes, and one of them became the valedictorian of his ninth-grade junior high school graduating class as well as the graduating class of his senior high school.

The results in the Washington School were similar to those described for the Jefferson School. This can be seen in Table 5-5.

On the Metropolitan Intermediate Reading Test given in the sixth grade, these eight children had scores ranging from 8.0 to 11.2. Here too, none of these children had obtained IQs of 125 or higher on the Otis Beta Test and since no other intelligence test had been administered during the previous three years, these eight children were also ineligible.

In the Advanced Metropolitan Reading Test given in the ninth grade, the scores of these eight children ranged from 10.4 to 12.0 with a mean of 11.2. On the Pintner General Ability Intermediate Test administered

Table 5-5  Data for Achievers Lacking Minimum IQ for SP Program—Washington School

| | Elementary School | | | | | | Junior High School | | |
| | IQ | | | | Grade Score | | | Grade Score | |
| | Pintner-Cunningham | Otis Alpha | Otis Beta | Hemmon-Nelson | Metropolitan Intermediate Reading | Metropolitan Intermediate Mathematics | Pintner Intermediate IQ | Metropolitan Advanced Reading | Average—Major Subjects (%) |
|---|---|---|---|---|---|---|---|---|---|
| Grade: | 1 | 3 | 6 | 6 | 6 | 6 | 9 | 9 | 7–9 |
| Boys | | | | | | | | | |
| J.E. | 113 | 118 | 115 | 135 | 11.2 | 9.4 | 135 | 12.0 | 62.0 [a] |
| Girls | | | | | | | | | |
| P.M. | 104 | 108 | 107 | 126 | 8.5 | 8.7 | 129 | 11.2 | 65.4 |
| B.J. | 93 | 95 | 112 | 128 | 8.3 | 10.2 | 121 | 11.3 | 88.8 |
| B.D. | 120 | 109 | 107 | 125 | 9.2 | 10.0 | 99 | 11.7 | 78.3 |
| D.K. | 113 | 109 | 102 | 125 | 8.8 | 10.5 | 127 | 11.3 | 79.0 |
| M.S. | 113 | 98 | 115 | 125 | 9.7 | 10.5 | 130 | 11.1 | 78.4 |
| W.W. | 105 | 109 | 112 | 127 | 10.5 | 8.3 | 119 | 10.6 | 72.1 |
| M.F. | 126 | 117 | 117 | 127 | 8.0 | 10.6 | 130 | 10.4 | 76.1 |

[a] Did not meet requirements for diploma.

in the same year they obtained IQs which ranged from 99 to 135. Although three of these children obtained ratings of less than 125, in examining their general performance and achievement in junior high school one notes that all but two did comparatively well in junior high school judging from the ratings obtained. It was learned, however, that the child with the highest IQ and the highest reading grade score was graduated with a certificate rather than with a diploma because he had failed to pass his foreign language and mathematics subjects. This boy, whose teachers consistently reported his high potential, had a long history of underachievement. His academic performance and his behavior in high school were consistently poor and he dropped out of school in the eleventh grade.

It was gratifying to note that teachers' faith in the ability of most of these children was verified by their achievement in the junior high school. It is not suggested here that standards for admission be lowered. The data do indicate, however, that class performance and teacher judgment, if used along with achievement test scores and IQ, are more predictive of success than are test scores alone. Furthermore, enough is known about the validity of group intelligence test scores to raise serious questions about such rigid reliance upon them in selecting children for special placement.*

The one boy whose subsequent progress differed so greatly from all others in the group warrants some description:

Jimmy, a black child, was the tallest boy in his class and grade level from the time he entered kindergarten. In several of his elementary and junior high school classes, he was at least six inches taller than the next tallest boy, and at an early age he developed the typical slouch of self-conscious, tall children. His "drawing of myself" in the second grade showed a figure with legs as tall as stilts. In the third grade, he was as tall as his teacher. Although he never talked about his height, he was very reluctant to be in the class pictures that were taken annually.

Jimmy's parents were also very tall. His father, a federal civil service employee, was the disciplinarian in the family, although his mother seemed to share the role. When in the third grade, children were asked to invite their parents to accompany the class on a trip, Jimmy said, "I don't want my mother to come. She'll always be saying, 'Jimmy, don't do that.'" Jimmy had a brother two years older who was attending school but who had an incurable disease leading to eventual blindness. Understandably, he was the object of much con-

---

* Three years later, intelligence testing in New York City was discontinued, not because of the problems raised in this chapter but because of the alleged cultural bias of the tests.

cern and attention at home and was always described by his mother in glowing terms, whereas Jimmy was "stubborn, disobedient, always fighting."

In the kindergarten, Jimmy was described as shy, a "loner," but independent in play and in exploring new toys and materials. He was particularly interested in playing with blocks and was very creative in using them. Although he did not volunteer to participate in activities, his teacher indicated that he was fairly well adjusted and his mother reported that he liked school.

Early in the first grade he learned to read and he was frequently asked to read stories to the class, which he seemed to enjoy. From then on through the junior high school, Jimmy almost consistently received the highest reading scores on achievement tests. Along with this skill, however, came patterns of behavior which seemed to create problems. His second-grade teacher wrote, "If Jimmy isn't reading a book on the desk, he's reading under the desk. And if he isn't reading, he's playing with one of his small toys which he always carries with him. He never volunteers an answer and looks bored most of the time."

The same theme runs through six years of anecdotal material. "He always looks bored, never participates in discussion, never volunteers for anything. Never seems to be paying attention but always knows the answer when called on."

As early as the second grade, Jimmy began selecting the activities in which he would take part and when he tired of reading or playing with small toys, he would wander about the room. His third-grade teacher listed him as an adjustment problem who "cares about nothing, does not participate in group activities, is always playing with toys, but always knows the answer when called on. Is very capable but doesn't find the grade work challenging."

Jimmy's fourth-grade teacher also listed him as a problem and described him as "very intelligent, can accomplish a lot with little effort, very lackadaisical. Does not abide by class rules or procedures; when reprimanded once, he mumbled, 'My mother says I'm so big—a big dope.'"

In the same grade, the Project Assistant wrote, "While children are checking answers to math problems, Jimmy is reading a book. Teacher calls on him. Jimmy hesitates for a second and then gives the correct answer explaining it very ably. He seems able to read and to keep up with class work."

He kept forgetting an appointment for a Binet test which had been arranged for him but was finally tested and achieved an IQ score of 146. Nevertheless, both the learning and behavior pattern persisted through the ninth grade, and although he was in the Special Progress class, he did the minimum amount of work and failed to graduate with a diploma. Efforts to secure psychological assistance and guidance failed because both Jimmy and his mother did not cooperate. Jimmy went on to high school with his superior ability and his many problems and finally left school in the eleventh grade, when we lost contact with him.

This waste of ability and potential parallels many studies in underachievement. It is difficult to pinpoint the specific cause of Jimmy's problems. There were probably many factors, but it seems that he gradually accepted his parents' demeaning image of him, fitted himself into it, and acted accordingly.

With the exception of Jimmy, all the other children in both schools who originally or by retesting, qualified for admission into SP classes did well in junior and senior high schools and graduated one year ahead of their classmates. There are among them now several teachers, nurses, secretaries, men working in business offices, and two are now attending professional graduate schools.

All the data available support the conclusions drawn by Terman and Oden in their monumental studies which showed that intellectually gifted children can easily be accelerated one or two years without harmful effects. They point out, "gifted children who have been promoted more rapidly than is customary are as a group equal or superior to gifted non-accelerates in health and general adjustment, do better schoolwork, continue their education further, marry a little earlier, and are more successful in their later careers" (1947, p. 377). The conclusions are reiterated in a later volume (1959, p. 72).

## THE PROMISE OF GIFTEDNESS

Recurring interest in giftedness and talents and the concern for early identification and education of gifted children are too well known to require discussion here. The advent of Sputnick brought with it, either through anxiety or through self-evaluation, a realization of the vast human resources waiting to be developed in children who had potential. When the Russian satellite left its launching pad, it also lifted with it to a level of professional respectability concern for the gifted and their education.

As a matter of information, it might be pointed out that New York City's interest in the gifted preceded the Sputnick era by approximately three decades. The experimental work done at the Speyer School (New York City Board of Education, 1941) in the 1930s and classes for the intellectually gifted children in the elementary schools which have been in existence since that time represent modest efforts to develop potential and to provide better education for superior students. The investigation of talent and the validity of teachers' identifications was thus one of the project's goals which was taken for granted and which preceded Sputnick by several years.

It was recognized that one of the most valid measures of teachers' abilities to recognize intellectual giftedness could be obtained only before any intelligence tests had been administered. By February of 1955, when children had completed the first half of the first grade, teachers had already become sufficiently acquainted with their pupils so that they could make judgments in relation to grouping for teaching. Grouping was now being carried on for levels of reading readiness, for reading, and to some extent for the teaching of number work. At this time, teachers were asked to estimate the intelligence of their children and were given a scale in which each child was to be rated as being exceptional, bright, average, dull, possibly retarded. Lists of children with special talents were also elicited in this and all subsequent grades. Approximately half the children in both schools were considered average in intelligence. In the Jefferson School 40% of the children were judged by teachers to be above average; 53% of the children subsequently obtained IQs above 110. In the Washington School 21% were considered bright or exceptional; data obtained later from the Pintner-Cunningham Test showed that exactly 21% of the children in this school had IQs above 110.

In both schools, the three children with the highest IQs were identified not as exceptional, but as bright. One girl in the Washington School had an IQ of 139 and two girls in the Jefferson School obtained IQs of 157 and 164. This estimate by teachers conforms to observations made in other studies of gifted children. It has been noted frequently that children of very high IQ are not motivated sufficiently to display their abilities and thus are very often not among the highest achievers in their groups (Terman and Oden, 1947; Pegnato and Birch, 1959; Gallagher, 1964; Gold, 1965; Hauck and Freehill, 1972). It may also be that teachers' estimates of potential are influenced by the display of effort which less able pupils make. Children with the lowest IQs seem to have been identified much more readily than those of any other group. The dull and average, for the most part, were also properly placed.

Although teachers were asked in each subsequent year to estimate the intelligence of their children in accordance with the scale just described, it would have been unrealistic to ignore the fact that their judgments were frequently influenced by their knowledge of IQ scores. Some teachers emphasized the fact that they were considering potentials, and as was noted in Chapter Four, they seriously questioned obtained IQ scores that were inconsistent with classroom performance or their own intuitive estimate of potential. In general, however, correlations between teachers' judgment, IQ, and classroom performance increased as children advanced through the elementary grades.

It thus became difficult to measure teacher ability to identify intellectual giftedness. Using admission to the SP classes at the end of the sixth grade as a criterion for measuring this ability does not altogether solve the problem. As was explained previously, admission to these classes was open only to those children who obtained IQs of 125 or higher and who, in the sixth grade, achieved grade scores of 8.0 or higher in mathematics and reading achievement tests.

In the Jefferson School, 23 boys qualified for admission to the SP classes or for acceleration; of these, 20 had been identified at least once as being intellectually gifted. Of the 14 girls who qualified, 11 had been so identified. Only one boy and one girl who had been rated as intellectually gifted failed to qualify.

In the Washington School, 10 children who had been judged at some time to be intellectually gifted were ineligible, but all who were admitted had been identified in at least one grade as being intellectually gifted or as possessing some special talent. In both schools, identification by one teacher had limited reliability, but when three or more different teachers judged a child to be intellectually gifted, prediction for admission to the accelerated program was absolute. Also of interest is the fact that every child who had been identified three or more times during his seven years in elementary school showed his superiority first as early as the first grade and no later than the second.

It should be emphasized here that when teachers were convinced of intellectual superiority, contradictory IQ scores did not influence teachers' judgments. For example, William obtained a Pintner-Cunningham IQ of 119 in Grade 1 and an Otis Alpha Quick Scoring IQ of 111 in Grade 3. He was, nevertheless, listed as intellectually gifted during four of his six years in the elementary grades and when he was given an individual Binet test in Grade 4 he obtained an IQ of 136. William was subsequently accelerated and also admitted to the SP classes in the junior high school from which he was graduated as valedictorian of his class. This validation of teacher judgment occurred in several other cases and perhaps points up the need to give teacher judgment greater weight in planning for the education of children.

As has been indicated, identification of giftedness was not limited to the field of the intellect. In discussions with teachers, the project staff helped to develop broader concepts of giftedness so as to include the many talents that children displayed. These discussions were structured to allow teachers to note any areas in which they thought children displayed superiority. As a result, many children were identified as having talents in art, dramatics, music, and athletics and also as being gifted in such areas as mechanical aptitude, construction, "social consciousness," leadership, "verbal expression," and sense of humor.

In the identification of children with these special talents, the picture is quite confused. For one thing, there is no simple way to verify teachers' identifications. Although the junior high schools did have special classes for musically gifted and artistically talented children, these were available only for those children who were not admitted to the SP classes. Many children of such talents went into the SP classes. Aptitude tests were given to those who were to go into special junior high school music or art classes, and of those who were admitted, as many had been previously identified as had not been so designated.

Consistent performance nevertheless was identified quite early. For example, those who had been listed three or more times as being talented in art or music or dramatics had displayed their special gifts by the time they had reached the second grade. It is also interesting to note that all the boys who had been singled out in the primary grades as being outstanding in athletics did well in junior high school athletics, two of the six winning a place on their junior high school basketball team.

It would seem, from our study, that the majority of the children who had special skills and aptitudes were, at some time in their elementary school years, identified. We will never know, however, how many children with special abilities were never fortunate enough to have been in the class of a teacher who was sensitive to their special area of superiority.

Consider the following incident:

In our quest to obtain specimens of our children's handwriting, various topics were used, as has been indicated in Chapter Three. The procedure in the fourth grade requested children to write on the topic "The Most Fun I Ever Had." The fourth grade in the Washington School consisted of seven classes, each grouped homogeneously, so that 4–1 was the brightest class on the grade and 4–7 was the slowest. Children in the slower classes of the grade had a good deal of difficulty in responding to the assignment which was given by the Project Assistant and was carried out immediately under her supervision. However, in one of these very slow classes a boy handed in the following paper which is quoted exactly as written.

THE MOST FUN I EVER HAD

At night when i nell down at my window. I see the moon as it brigtens the dark sky and the nightingale when it comes out to sing and the breeze began to blow the mighty sea agaist the dam. And when i hear those sounds I know its summer time.

During the assignment this boy had asked the Project Assistant whether he might make a drawing and write more. And so there followed a drawing and then this paragraph beneath the drawing.

THE MOST FUN I EVER HAD

I stand down at the sea shore at night. And feel the warm breeze as it go by. I hear the nightingale as it sings to me so nice, so sweet, so gay. I see the gray seas as it turns a dark blue. And when I have those feeling I know its summertime

We hurried to the teacher to find further examples of this boy's writing. All of his papers that were available were in keeping with the achievement of children in that slow class and not one of them showed the amazing sensitivity and skill found in these two paragraphs. Nor had any teacher ever listed him as having any gifts or talents.

What may we conclude from this incident, from this glimpse of talent? Perhaps it is unimportant that there are neither dams nor nightingales in New York City. What is important, however, is that here is a boy who was able to pluck from his visual or auditory environment those elements that kindled his creative talent and gave him an opportunity to react to his special sensitivities. It is distressing to note that normal classroom procedures never brought about any display or development of this talent. Unfortunately, this boy moved out of New York City and was lost to us.

It would seem from our study of potential that intellectual ability is most easily displayed and most readily identified in the normal school situation. The same cannot be said of other areas of giftedness or talents. All teachers seemed to be sensitive to their own areas of special skills or talents and therefore provided opportunities for expression, and were able to identify children who showed superiority. For example, in the first grade, one boy was identified as having mechanical aptitude. This was the only such identification made during the entire course of the study, and it was recorded by a teacher who was herself mechanically gifted. A few were sensitive to areas other than the one in which they possessed skills and were perceptive to children's superiority in these areas.

We must also conclude that unless a teacher provides opportunities for the display of gifts and talents, such gifts and talents will never be shown. Where a program is so sterile that children rarely have an opportunity to sing, to paint, or to act, no one will be identified as having special skills in these areas. Where a teacher carried on a good art program, many more children were identified as being talented in art. Where a good music program or science program was in progress, children had an opportunity to display their special gifts and talents in music or science. And, conversely, where any program was minimized or carried on in a perfunctory, uninspiring manner, few children were found to have any talents.

It might be advisable to reevaluate the self-contained classroom and consider the possibility of having specialists communicate to the children their own enthusiasm and talents in these various areas. We can only conjecture how many children must pass through our schools without ever experiencing the excitement and gratification that comes with the realization of a talent, and without teacher-recognition and approval of superiority, however slender and small.

It is interesting that the many special abilities and talents that were identified in the elementary school were, with the few exceptions previously mentioned, rarely sustained or demonstrated in the senior high school. The only consistent performers were those who had been identified as intellectually gifted and whose early promise was fulfilled. Visits to high schools and examination of high school records showed our children joining clubs and pursuing interests which could not have been predicted in their early years. Furthermore, hobbies and interests in the years following high school were more closely associated with high school interests than with elementary school interests and skills.

Observations and discussions with children seemed to show that the selection of clubs and activities in high school was determined more often than not by the variety offered in any one school, by peer interests and pressures, and by the enthusiasm for his subject that a skillful teacher was able to convey to his students.

# CHAPTER SIX

## Adjustment

### CHILDREN WITH PROBLEMS

It is with considerable hesitation and timidity that we approach the problem of adjustment. What do adjustment and maladjustment mean to teachers? Do they mean the same to an authoritarian teacher as they do to a permissive teacher? Asking teachers to identify children who are well and poorly adjusted presents obvious difficulties. In a paper presented before the American Educational Research Association, Ward (1963) stated: "Although there are good reasons to measure intangibles such as social and emotional adjustment, ratings by untrained teachers do not seem to be very profitable." We cannot assume that the 66 elementary school teachers and the many junior high school teachers with whom our staff worked in the course of the study were completely "untrained." Certainly the teacher-staff conferences in which instruments and children were discussed provided a good deal of training, sufficient to involve teachers in the investigation of adjustment.

In order to identify children who were having adjustment problems in the elementary school, two instruments were used. One of these, which teachers submitted in November and March of each year, consisted simply of a listing of such children with comments concerning the kinds of

**67**

problems they presented. It was hoped that this procedure would provide some information concerning children who remained problems in the grade and those who presented initial problems before they were able to accept teacher standards and before teachers were able to accept children's behavior. Almost all children who were reported in November appeared again on the March lists. The few who did not showed no consistency or pattern in their difficulties, and none of them reappeared on lists in any subsequent grade.

The other instrument, used toward the close of each school year, was a 5-point scale on which teachers rated all their children on their degree of adjustment. A rating of 1 was given to children who were considered very well adjusted, and a rating of 5 to those considered very poorly adjusted, with provisions for extra comments for those children requiring, in the teacher's opinion, clinical observation and diagnosis.

Examination of teacher responses did not confirm Ward's statement but did present some interesting contrasts. In spite of any understandings that may have been developed during the course of this study, a teacher's interpretation of adjustment was more often than not directly influenced by the kind of school in which she found herself and by the nature of the class she had at the time. This can readily be understood. Where a teacher's experiences have been limited to a so-called difficult school such as the Washington School, the problems of classroom control and management may be so overwhelming that only those children who create such problems and who interfere with the authority of the teacher or with the proper functioning of the class are identified as being maladjusted.

There is no doubt that courses in classroom management, mental hygiene, and conferences with the project staff were invaluable for teachers, but the daily attrition of difficult classroom management problems caused them to focus their attention on the children who were most disturbing. Thus, whereas teachers in the Washington School recognized introverted behavior and attempted to deal with it, they tended to identify only those who were most troublesome to the class and to the teacher when they were asked to list the names of children with adjustment problems. Leacock points out that "from the teacher's viewpoint, two or three openly rebellious children are all that is needed to command her constant attention and dissipate her energies. Such children dominate the scene" (1969, p. 154).

In this school, therefore, the boys and girls most frequently listed as adjustment problems were generally described as being "aggressive, hostile, unable to take criticism, unable to control behavior, irritable, interfering with the rights of others."

In the Jefferson School, children came with the usual cultural patterns, standards, and attitudes which the literature indicates are found in middle-income areas, and as a result, their preparation and motivation for school and learning were different. Furthermore, "the goals for conduct and the type of behavior emphasized as either good or bad are quite different in middle and in low-income schools" (Leacock, 1969, p. 157).

Thus problems of classroom management were comparatively minor in this school and teachers had the time and greater opportunity to identify their problem children in broader terms. Although some children in this school did interfere with classroom procedures, many more children here were identified as having personal problems. For example, problems in the Jefferson School were described more often as "hyperactive, socially immature, sucks thumb, restless, needs attention, oversensitive, shy, feels rejected, unusually quiet, unhappy, doesn't work up to capacity, overprotected, timid." As a result, many more pupils were listed as problems over a seven-year period in the Jefferson School than in the Washington School. It would, however, be unrealistic as well as inaccurate to conclude that there were more children with problems in the Jefferson School, as Table 6-1 seems to indicate.

**Table 6-1    Incidence of Reported Maladjustment in the Elementary School**

|  | Number of Times Reported, Grades 1–6 | Boys | | Girls | | Total | |
|---|---|---|---|---|---|---|---|
|  |  | N | Percentage | N | Percentage | N | Percentage |
| Jefferson School | Three or more | 22 | 47.8 | 16 | 41.0 | 38 | 44.7 |
|  | Twice | 8 | 17.4 | 5 | 12.8 | 13 | 15.3 |
|  | Never or once | 16 | 34.8 | 18 | 46.2 | 34 | 40.0 |
|  | Total | 46 | 100.0 | 39 | 100.0 | 85 | 100.0 |
| Washington School | Three or more | 8 | 25.0 | 7 | 14.6 | 15 | 18.8 |
|  | Twice | 5 | 15.6 | 5 | 10.4 | 10 | 12.5 |
|  | Never or once | 19 | 59.4 | 36 | 75.0 | 55 | 68.7 |
|  | Total | 32 | 100.0 | 48 | 100.0 | 80 | 100.0 |

The responses of our teachers warrant some interesting comparisons with the Wickman (1928) and subsequent studies of teacher attitudes toward pupil behavior. Wickman asked a group of 511 elementary school teachers to rank a list of 50 school behavior problems in order of their degree of seriousness. Thirty clinical psychologists were also asked to rank the problems, but from the standpoint of mental hygiene. Teachers ranked as most serious those behaviors that were aggressive and most likely to interfere with instruction or disrupt the class, whereas the mental hygienists ranked all types of withdrawal behavior as most serious.

Mitchell (1942) replicated the Wickman study and found that teachers and clinicians had moved closer together in their concepts of problem behavior but that teachers were still concerned with conforming behavior in the classroom. A similar study by Stouffer (1952) again showed greater consensus between the two groups but continuing teacher concern for acceptable classroom behavior. Stouffer notes that teachers and clinicians have different responsibilities for children, and that community expectations and group teaching situations determine for the teacher minimum behavior standards without which effective teaching and learning cannot take place.

In 1955, when this study was already under way, Hunter (1957) sought to determine how teachers viewed the seriousness of problems originally presented by Wickman in 1928. He found still greater concurrence with Wickman's clinicians but persisting teacher concern with aggressive classroom behavior. He also found some differences in attitudes of teachers of different sex, race, education, and teaching experience, and greater agreement between clinicians and teachers holding higher degrees.

A study by Tolor et al. (1967) used the Staten Island Behavioral Scale, which contains 295 behavioral items. It was administered to 118 elementary school teachers and 23 clinical psychologists with instructions to rate each item as either normal or abnormal behavior. The two groups differed in 22% of the items. "The teachers tended to regard almost all of the differentiating behavioral descriptions abnormal whereas the psychologists perceived them to be normal. Teacher experience was found to be a significant variable with inexperienced teachers differing more from the psychologists . . . than experienced teachers" (p. 175).

There are some obvious differences between the tasks presented to the teachers in these studies and those required of the teachers in our study. In the studies just described, teachers were asked to react to specific behavior patterns and to indicate their relative importance. It was essentially an intellectual task that could be carried on dispassionately and objectively. In working with our teachers, we talked about children, not behavior, and we gave no suggestions of categories of behavior. In responding, teachers talked of *specific* children in the framework of the daily experience and the frustrations of classroom teaching.

The variable of experience did not seem to play a part in teachers' descriptions of maladjusted children. Teachers in the Jefferson School, with one exception, had all been teaching less than ten years and several had only one or two years of experience. They were all white men and women. In the Washington School the teachers, who were black and white women and a few white men, had far more experience. Yet, contrary to the findings of Hunter's study, there was general agreement among these teachers regardless of sex, race, or education. Furthermore, the Washington School teachers, with more years of teaching experience, listed problems entirely consistent with those of Wickman's teachers, whereas Jefferson School teachers agreed more closely with his mental hygienists. It might be interesting to replicate the Wickman or Hunter study and examine the variable of the type of school in which the respondent teaches.

The use of lists of children with adjustment problems and, in addition, an adjustment rating scale produced an interesting paradox. There were several children in each school who appeared quite consistently on lists of adjustment problems but who received comparatively good ratings on the general adjustment rating scales. Examination of the specific cases, however, indicates that many children who were identified as having personal problems were nevertheless able to adjust well to the typical classroom situation and to make suitable progress in their studies. Redl and Wattenberg (1951) explain this paradox and point out that it is possible for a child to be either well adjusted or normal and still be in need of the special attention of a teacher or even of a school psychologist. They explain further that the child who reacts to the everyday give-and-take of life in a typical school by withdrawing, keeping to himself, avoiding contact with others may have developed a mode of adjustment. He may even find this adjustment satisfying, they say, in that he is able to maintain anxiety at a level that is "comfortable" most of the time; yet it is obvious that this is not a healthy kind of behavior.

For purposes of this study, an adjustment problem is defined as a child with problems who has been reported by three or more teachers in the elementary school. (We are accepting teacher terminology and general usage in using the term "problem" to refer to a *child* exhibiting behavior problems.) This criterion is arbitrarily chosen, but when a child has been identified as being maladjusted by approximately half of the teachers to whom he has been exposed, it can be assumed that the appearance of a problem is not accidental. It is felt that the identification of a problem by only one or two of seven teachers can reasonably be ignored and can be attributed to the difficulties of pupil-teacher adjustment in a particular situation or to a child's temporary problems.

In identifying our adjustment problems, we knowingly encountered further difficulties. Of a total of 71 teachers who had been asked to submit their lists of adjustment problems over a seven-year period in the elementary schools, there were probably a few who were threatened by this request and who considered such identification an admission of their own weaknesses. In spite of staff efforts to reassure all teachers with whom they worked, there were, no doubt, several children whose identification was omitted in certain years of their school life when, nevertheless, satisfactory adjustment had not been achieved.

A similar problem arose from a somewhat different situation. In discussing our children, one very able and perceptive teacher stated: "I'm sure that George could be a difficult problem in the classroom but I have learned to anticipate the incidents and situations that provoke him and I can maneuver accordingly. He could very well be a problem but I cannot say that he has been one and I am therefore not listing him." A cursory examination of George's record, therefore, would make it appear that his problems disappeared in this grade although we know that they really did not.

In the growing concern with juvenile delinquency, much has been written about the need for identifying problem behavior and delinquency at an early age. When we examine the records of the 53 children who were considered problems by three or more of their elementary school teachers, we find that all but three of them had been identified as such by the time they had completed the third grade. By the end of the first grade, 29 of the 53 had already revealed problems of maladjustment. These data are shown in Table 6-2.

One can assume that the proportion of problem cases identified in the kindergarten or first grade in the Washington School would have been much greater had there been less mobility there. Many children in that school who had been reported as problems in kindergarten and first grade moved and were transferred out of the school. Furthermore, of these, three boys and two girls had problems of such severity that they were transferred to state institutions or to special classes in special schools at some time during the primary grades.

Throughout the study, teachers did not know which children had been identified as problems in previous grades. Although they did have

Table 6-2   Grade of Initial Identification of Adjustment Problems

|                    | Grade Identified | | | | | |
|--------------------|------|------|------|------|------|------|
|                    | K    | 1    | 2    | 3    | 4    | N    |
| Jefferson School   |      |      |      |      |      |      |
| Boys               | 11   | 4    | 3    | 3    | 1    | 22   |
| Girls              | 3    | 7    | 4    | 1    | 1    | 16   |
| Total              | 14   | 11   | 7    | 4    | 2    | 38   |
| Washington School  |      |      |      |      |      |      |
| Boys               | 3    | 1    | 1    | 3    | 0    | 8    |
| Girls              | 0    | 0    | 3    | 3    | 1    | 7    |
| Total              | 3    | 1    | 4    | 6    | 1    | 15   |
| Total N            | 17   | 12   | 11   | 10   | 3    | 53   |

*Note:* Children reported for the first time beyond the fourth grade do not meet criteria for inclusion.

cumulative record cards for all of their children, these cards frequently did not contain notations of problem behavior, nor did these cards require the type of information which we were seeking.

Neither was there a "catch-all" factor operating in the accuracy of teachers' identifications. Although an occasional teacher did report a large number of children as problems, our total group of 71 teachers generally seemed to be conservative in making such identifications. Table 6-3 shows the total number of adjustment problems reported for each grade. It also indicates (contrary to popular conception) that teachers in the more difficult Washington School did not regard as many children as problems as did teachers in the "advantaged" Jefferson School.

In an attempt to examine more intensively children with adjustment problems, those reported were categorized as aggressive and nonaggressive. The aggressive ones usually involved others in their difficulties and included children who punched, talked out in class, interfered with the rights of others, bullied, and stole. The nonaggressive did not affect others in the class but included children who were shy, withdrawn, needed encouragement, and showed other symptoms of introverted behavior. This classification, however, produced no data of any significance. There was little if any difference between the two groups in intelligence, achievement, and other characteristics examined.

Table 6-3  Total Number of Children Reported as Problems in Each Grade in the Elementary School

| Grade: | K | 1 | 2 | 3 | 4 | 5 | 6 |
|---|---|---|---|---|---|---|---|
| Jefferson School | | | | | | | |
| Number of teachers | 3 | 4 | 4 | 4 | 3 | 3 | 3 |
| Boys, $N = 46$ | 11 (11) [a] | 17 (14) | 18 (15) | 16 (13) | 20 (15) | 25 (20) | 18 (15) |
| Girls, $N = 39$ | 3 (3) | 11 (10) | 13 (11) | 11 (7) | 14 (11) | 16 (13) | 12 (11) |
| Total   85 | 14 (14) | 28 (24) | 31 (26) | 27 (20) | 34 (26) | 41 (33) | 30 (26) |
| Washington School | | | | | | | |
| Number of teachers | 2 | 5 | 6 | 7 | 7 | 7 | 7 |
| Boys, $N = 32$ | 3 (3) | 4 (3) | 7 (4) | 8 (8) | 11 (7) | 12 (6) | 9 (4) |
| Girls, $N = 48$ | 1 (0) | 2 (0) | 4 (3) | 7 (4) | 12 (7) | 13 (7) | 7 (6) |
| Total   80 | 4 (3) | 4 (3) | 11 (7) | 15 (12) | 23 (14) | 25 (13) | 16 (10) |

[a] Numbers in parentheses are cumulative and indicate those who eventually had been reported three or more times.

Let us now examine the adjustment patterns of our problem children. Tables 6-4 and 6-5 present a variety of data for them.

These tables indicate that the seemingly subjective judgment of teachers concerning the maladjustment of their children has great validity. As can be seen from Table 6-3, most of the children reported as having adjustment problems in any one of the early grades remained problems and were subsequently reported by two or more other teachers. Furthermore, all but three of the children who fall into the category of adjustment problems (Tables 6-4 and 6-5) displayed their difficulties before the end of the third grade. In other words, in our basic population, most of the children who were reported as problems three or more times during their elementary school years had already been identified in the primary grades and did not "grow out of it" as they matured. On the contrary, there seemed to be a continuation or an intensification of the problem. Furthermore, incidence of adjustment problems did not show a sex difference and did not support the many studies that showed that behavior problems are more than twice as common in boys as in girls (Tanner and Lindgren, 1971; Rubin and Balow, 1971; Glavin, 1972).

Let us now examine the relationship between maladjustment and the variety of measures that were obtained in this study. How do maladjusted children compare with the well adjusted in intelligence, achievement, and other measures? We define maladjustment as we did before, that is, being reported three or more times for having presented problems of behavior in the classroom. Well-adjusted children are those who have been reported only once or never at all. For purposes of comparison we are omitting children on the borderline who were reported twice.

In the Jefferson School, 38 of the 85 basic children were reported as problems three or more times, while in the Washington School 15 of the 80 basic children were so reported. Data for the well and poorly adjusted are presented in Table 6-6.

If we compare the mean IQs of the problem children with those of the well-adjusted children we find that there is no significant difference in either school on the Pintner-Cunningham Test given in the first grade and on the Otis Alpha Test given in the third grade. On the Otis Beta Test given in the sixth grade there was a significant superiority in the mean of the well-adjusted group in the Jefferson School compared with that of the problem group, whereas in the Washington School there was again no significant difference shown in intelligence.

In examining achievement scores, however, we find the maladjusted children in both schools score consistently, although only slightly below the mean of those who were not adjustment problems. The difference

Table 6-4 Elementary School Adjustment and Achievement Ratings for Children with Problems—Jefferson School

| | Reported as Problem by Teacher | | | | | | | General [a] Adjustment Rating Scale—Median | IQ | | | Reading | | | Mathematics |
|---|---|---|---|---|---|---|---|---|---|---|---|---|---|---|---|
| | | | | | | | | | PC [b] | Otis Alpha | Otis Beta | NYRR [c] Percentile | Metropolitan [a] Grade Score | Metropolitan [a] Grade Score | Metropolitan [a] Grade Score |
| Grade: | K | 1 | 2 | 3 | 4 | 5 | 6 | 1-6 | 1 | 3 | 6 | 1 | 3 | 6 | 6 |
| Boys | | | | | | | | | | | | | | | |
| B.R. | X | | | | | | X | 3.0 | 112 | 110 | 123 | 90 | 5.3 | 9.9 | 9.0 |
| D.B. | X | X | X | X | X | X | X | 5.0 | 112 | 102 | 121 | 90 | 3.4 | 6.7 | 7.7 |
| F.R. | | X | | X | X | X | X | 2.0 | 113 | 113 | 138 | 90 | 5.0 | 9.8 | 8.5 |
| G.G. | X | X | | X | X | X | X | 4.0 | 101 | 99 | 103 | 30 | 2.3 | 4.8 | 5.9 |
| H.R. | | | X | X | X | X | X | 3.0 | 107 | 94 | 100 | 90 | 2.3 | 6.5 | 5.7 |
| M.I. | | X | X | X | X | X | X | 4.0 | 104 | 88 | 124 | 80 | 3.5 | 8.4 | 5.6 |
| P.A. | X | X | X | X | X | X | X | 4.0 | 105 | 106 | 120 | 80 | 4.2 | 10.5 | 10.0 |
| S.J. | X | X | X | | X | | X | 3.5 | 126 | 119 | 131 | 80 | 4.2 | 7.7 | 8.2 |
| S.H. | X | | X | | X | X | X | 3.5 | 96 | 87 | 89 | 40 | 1.5 | 5.5 | 5.4 |
| F.H. | X | X | X | | | X | X | 3.0 | 99 | 92 | 109 | 30 | 2.9 | 6.7 | 8.8 |
| S.N. | | | | X | X | X | | 2.5 | 89 | 88 | 90 | 40 | 3.2 | 5.4 | 5.3 |
| S.B. | | X | X | | | X | X | 4.5 | 93 | 86 | 75 | 40 | 2.1 | 3.5 | 6.6 |
| S.I. | X | X | X | | | | X | 2.5 | 106 | 101 | 101 | 70 | 4.5 | 8.1 | 6.1 |
| S.V. | | | X | X | | X | X | 3.0 | 89 | 88 | 82 | 80 | 2.7 | 4.4 | 6.0 |
| W.J. | | X | | | | X | X | 2.0 | 144 | 119 | 124 | 90 | 4.7 | 7.2 | 7.1 |
| D.Y. | X | X | X | X | X | X | | 3.5 | 95 | 98 | 80 | 30 | 2.3 | 4.5 | 6.9 |
| P.J. | | X | X | X | | | | 2.0 | 112 | 93 | 112 | 80 | 3.9 | 6.5 | 8.7 |
| R.M. | | X | X | | | | X | 1.5 | 94 | 101 | 115 | 10 | 4.3 | 9.0 | 9.5 |

| | | Rating[a] | [b] | [c] | | % | | | |
|---|---|---|---|---|---|---|---|---|---|
| S.S. | X X X | 3.5 | 135 | 123 | 131 | 90 | 4.5 | 9.7 | 8.7 |
| S.P. | X  X X X | 2.0 | 123 | 119 | 134 | 90 | 5.1 | 9.8 | 10.0 |
| W.H. | X X X X | 3.5 | 119 | 111 | — | 50 | 5.4 | Accelerated | |
| O.A. | X X  X | 3.0 | 109 | 99 | 127 | 70 | 3.8 | 7.6 | 7.3 |
| Girls | | | | | | | | | |
| B.B. | X  X X X | 2.5 | 113 | 107 | 127 | 80 | 4.6 | 9.3 | 9.3 |
| B.E. | X X X X | 3.0 | 99 | 111 | 102 | 40 | 4.5 | 8.0 | 8.4 |
| M.D. | X X X | 4.5 | 85 | 74 | 82 | 40 | 3.0 | 5.1 | 3.8 |
| N.J. | X X X X | 2.0 | 85 | 102 | 94 | 70 | 3.6 | 5.5 | 5.8 |
| S.M. | X X X | 1.5 | 115 | 91 | 92 | 80 | 3.1 | 6.3 | 6.9 |
| A.S. | X X X  X X X | 2.5 | 120 | 109 | 121 | 90 | 4.3 | 10.5 | 9.2 |
| B.L. | X X X  X X X | 3.5 | 121 | 107 | 109 | 70 | 3.6 | 6.8 | 6.9 |
| E.B. | X X  X | 2.0 | 145 | 107 | 135 | 90 | 5.2 | 9.2 | 10.3 |
| H.M. | X  X | 2.0 | 114 | 101 | 125 | 70 | 4.6 | 8.1 | 6.4 |
| J.L. | X  X X X | 2.5 | 96 | 95 | 95 | 40 | 3.3 | 5.1 | 7.5 |
| J.B. | X X X  X X X | 3.5 | 88 | 89 | 88 | 10 | 2.4 | 5.0 | 4.7 |
| M.L. | X X X X  X X X | 4.5 | 112 | 87 | 112 | 80 | 3.3 | 6.9 | 5.3 |
| P.L. | X X X  X | 3.0 | 112 | 103 | 103 | 60 | 3.4 | 6.6 | 6.0 |
| S.N. | X | 3.0 | 112 | 109 | 102 | — | 2.7 | 4.3 | 6.0 |
| S.R. | X  X  X X X | 2.0 | 109 | 127 | 110 | 50 | 3.4 | 5.8 | 8.0 |
| H.A. | X X X | 3.0 | 82 | 79 | 91 | 10 | 3.1 | 5.0 | 6.3 |
| N = 22 boys, 16 girls | Mean = 3.2 | | 107.7 | 100.9 | 108.6 | 62 | 3.7 | 7.1 | 7.2 |

[a] 1 = very well adjusted; 5 = very poorly adjusted.
[b] Pintner-Cunningham Primary Test.
[c] New York Reading Readiness Test.
[d] Metropolitan Reading or Mathematics Tests—Primary, Elementary, Intermediate—as appropriate to the grade level.

**Table 6-5  Elementary School Adjustment and Achievement Ratings for Children with Problems—Washington School**

| Grade | Reported as Problem by Teacher K | 1 | 2 | 3 | 4 | 5 | 6 | General[a] Adjustment Rating Scale—Median 1-6 | IQ PC[b] 1 | IQ Otis Alpha 3 | IQ Otis Beta 6 | NYRR[c] Percentile 1 | Reading Metropolitan[d] Grade Score 3 | Reading 6 | Mathematics Metropolitan[d] Grade Score 6 |
|---|---|---|---|---|---|---|---|---|---|---|---|---|---|---|---|
| **Boys** | | | | | | | | | | | | | | | |
| H.W. | X | X | X | X | | | | 2.0 | 106 | 81 | 87 | 10 | 1.3 | 4.4 | 5.8 |
| J.E. | X | | | X | X | | | 2.5 | 113 | 118 | 115 | 90 | 5.3 | 11.2 | 9.9 |
| S.M. | | | X | X | | X | | 3.0 | 112 | 96 | 95 | 40 | 2.0 | 4.5 | 5.6 |
| W.R. | | | X | X | X | X | | 2.0 | 77 | 90 | 82 | 10 | 2.6 | 4.0 | 5.1 |
| B.L. | | X | X | X | X | X | X | 5.0 | 103 | 124 | 103 | — | 3.3 | 6.7 | 7.3 |
| K.J. | X | X | X | X | X | X | X | 4.5 | 103 | 93 | 87 | 70 | 2.5 | 3.9 | 5.9 |
| P.J. | X | X | X | X | X | X | X | 4.0 | 78 | 87 | 77 | 30 | 2.6 | 3.4 | 5.0 |
| M.V. | | | X | X | X | X | | 4.0 | 99 | 103 | 96 | — | 3.2 | 6.3 | 5.9 |
| **Girls** | | | | | | | | | | | | | | | |
| S.C. | | X | X | X | | | | 1.5 | 90 | 95 | 107 | 90 | 3.7 | 8.0 | 5.6 |
| C.B. | | | X | X | X | | | 2.5 | 81 | 69 | 82 | 0 | 3.1 | 4.6 | 4.4 |
| D.B. | X | | | X | X | X | | 4.5 | 94 | 92 | 95 | 40 | 2.8 | 4.8 | 5.2 |
| M.M. | | | X | X | X | X | X | 2.0 | 103 | 99 | 114 | 70 | 4.2 | 7.2 | 5.9 |
| M.J. | | | X | X | X | X | X | 4.0 | 74 | 80 | 95 | 0 | 2.3 | 3.5 | 3.6 |
| S.T. | | X | X | X | X | X | | 3.5 | 101 | 96 | 93 | 20 | 3.8 | 6.4 | 6.0 |
| W.G. | X | | | X | X | X | | 3.0 | 90 | 94 | 113 | 50 | 4.1 | 6.7 | 6.8 |
| N = 8 boys, 7 girls | | | | | | | | Mean = 3.2 | 94.9 | 94.5 | 96.1 | 40 | 3.1 | 5.7 | 5.9 |

[a] 1 = very well adjusted; 5 = very poorly adjusted.
[b] Pintner-Cunningham Primary Test.
[c] New York Reading Readiness Test.
[d] Metropolitan Reading or Mathematics Test—Primary, Elementary, Intermediate—as appropriate to the grade level.

Table 6-6   Comparison of Elementary School Test Scores between Poorly Adjusted and Well-Adjusted Children

| | Number of Times Reported | |
|---|---|---|
| | Three or More | Never or Once |
| Jefferson School | (N = 38) | (N = 34) |
| Intelligence tests | | |
| Pintner-Cunningham—Grade 1 | IQ = 107.7 | 105.0 |
| Otis Alpha—Grade 3 | IQ = 100.9 | 103.6 |
| Otis Beta—Grade 6 | IQ = 108.6 | 116.2 [b] |
| Reading tests | | |
| New York Reading Readiness— Grade 1 | Percentile =  63.0 | 80.0 [c] |
| Metropolitan—Grade 3 | Grade score =  3.7 | 4.3 [c] |
| Metropolitan—Grade 6 | Grade score =  7.3 | 7.9 |
| Mathematics test | | |
| Metropolitan—Grade 6 | Grade score =  7.2 | 8.4 [c] |
| Adjustment | | |
| General Adjustment Rating Scale for Grades 1–6 | Rating [a] =  3.2 | 1.5 |
| Washington School | (N = 15) | (N = 55) |
| Intelligence tests | | |
| Pintner-Cunningham—Grade 1 | IQ =  94.9 | 94.1 |
| Otis Alpha—Grade 3 | IQ =  94.5 | 94.7 |
| Otis Beta—Grade 6 | IQ =  96.0 | 98.2 |
| Reading tests | | |
| New York Reading Readiness— Grade 1 | Percentile =  40.0 | 59.6 [b] |
| Metropolitan—Grade 3 | Grade score =  3.1 | 3.5 |
| Metropolitan—Grade 6 | Grade score =  5.7 | 5.9 |
| Mathematics test | | |
| Metropolitan—Grade 6 | Grade score =  5.9 | 6.8 [b] |
| Adjustment | | |
| General Adjustment Rating Scale for Grades 1–6 | Rating [a] =  3.2 | 1.5 |

Note: All scores reported are mean scores.

[a] 1 = very well adjusted; 5 = very poorly adjusted.

[b] Significant at the .05 level of confidence.

[c] Significant at the .01 level of confidence.

was somewhat greater in the Jefferson School than in the Washington School where it was only slight. This applies to all reading tests given in the first, third, and sixth grades, and to the sixth-grade mathematics test. In both schools the greatest difference in scores occurred in the first grade on the New York Reading Readiness Test which was given before the beginning of formal reading. Here the mean percentile rating of the maladjusted (and this included those who were not regarded as problems until years later) was 17 points below the well adjusted in the Jefferson School and 19.6 points below in the Washington School. Just why the New York Reading Readiness Test should have served as so sensitive an indicator and predictor of maladjustment cannot be determined.

The manual of this test states that the percentile ratings "give only a small part of the information needed for judging the child's readiness for book reading. In addition to test scores, a study of his general development is necessary. This involves an appraisal of his physical, mental, social, and emotional functioning; of his language development and of his experiential background" (New York City Board of Education, 1947, p. 3). Teachers are asked to rate the children satisfactory or unsatisfactory in these areas. Approximately the same proportion of children from each group was considered entirely satisfactory or unsatisfactory and no single area seemed to be more significant for the maladjusted than for the well adjusted.

One must be cautious in drawing the logical conclusion that early difficulty with reading produces subsequent maladjustment and problems in school. It may very well be one of the factors. Nevertheless, the children with adjustment problems in the study included both the best and the poorest readers. In the Jefferson School, four of the ten best readers as measured by the Metropolitan Achievement Test in Reading given in the sixth grade had been identified as adjustment problems, as were nine of the ten poorest readers. In the Washington School, one of the ten best readers and four of the ten poorest readers had also been listed three or more times as problems.

In the sixth-grade mathematics test the difference in the mean grade score of the well-adjusted and maladjusted groups was significant in both schools; in the Jefferson School there was a difference of one year and two months between the means of the two groups, and in the Washington School there was a nine-month difference.

On the General Adjustment Rating Scale, in both schools, differences between the well and the poorly adjusted were considerable, as would be expected.

In attempting to draw generalizations, all other data were examined but much of it showed no distinction between the maladjusted and the well adjusted. For example, on sociometric measures obtained in the elementary school there were children of both groups who were consistently chosen by their peers, as well as those who were never or rarely chosen throughout the grades.

Approximately the same proportion of children in each group came from disrupted homes. The maladjusted children presented no greater psychophysical or physical problems, such as stammering or orthopedic handicaps, than did the others. Consistent extremes in both height and weight were found in both groups, and left-handedness did not seem to distinguish the two. There was, in fact, a larger percentage of left-handed children among the well adjusted, and as far as we could tell from observations of children and interviews with parents, there were probably few if any forced changes in handedness prior or subsequent to admission to school.

Ordinal position in the family was also examined. Breckenridge and Vincent (1960) review the literature on the subject and note that it agrees fairly well that oldest children are somewhat more delinquent than the other children. Kaplan summarizes several studies and concludes that "firstborn children tend to have more adjustment problems" (1965, p. 87). If we apply this conclusion to adjustment rather than delinquency, it does not seem to be characteristic of our population, whose ordinal position seemed to be unrelated to adjustment.

In an effort to determine whether the maladjusted children also presented problems at home, questions concerning home adjustment were included on questionnaires given to parents in the first, third, and sixth grades of the study. In the first grade it was asked simply as "How does he/she get along at home?" In the third and sixth grades the question was, "Does he/she present any problems at home?"

It is very difficult to determine from responses to the questionnaires the extent and types of poor adjustment at home as reported by parents. Most statements were very general. Sibling rivalry was mentioned most frequently, but the seriousness of the problem could not be determined. Furthermore, parents of the well adjusted as well as of the poorly adjusted reported their children as presenting problems at home in almost equal numbers. There may be some significance in the fact that in the Washington School many more parents of children who were problems in school consistently failed to answer the question about home adjustment. This may suggest parental reluctance to reveal facts concerning their children's behavior at home.

It was, unfortunately, not possible to continue obtaining such detailed data during the junior and senior high school years. Since most of the children in the Jefferson School attended the same junior and senior high schools, more data were available for them than for those who had attended the Washington School. Furthermore, the one Project Assistant who was retained was the one known to them and it was thus possible to continue the close and cooperative relationship that had been established.

The instruments that had been used in the elementary grades to measure adjustment were continued for the Jefferson School children in their junior high school. Because of the departmental type of program where children have different teachers for each subject, ratings were obtained from many more teachers. For the remaining 31 children who had been rated as problems in the elementary school, the mean rating on the General Adjustment Scale for the junior high school grades was 3.0 as compared with 3.2, which they had received in the elementary school. The majority of these children showed a slight improvement, a few remained the same, and only two received lower ratings.

This improvement in adjustment may be more apparent than real. It may be due to the fact that in the departmentalized program of the junior high school both teachers and children had an opportunity every 45 minutes to begin again. Thus a poorly adjusted child may not be considered as difficult or indicate his problems as much in a short period of time as he might when he is with one teacher for an entire day, as was the case in the elementary school.

Detailed studies of some children with adjustment problems will illustrate the persistence of behavior patterns. As indicated, children reported as maladjusted in the Washington School generally were those who presented problems of classroom behavior. As a result, case studies of these children have running through all of them a common thread of aggressive, annoying behavior.

Paul was reported as an adjustment problem by each of his elementary school teachers. He lived with an aunt and uncle. No information was available concerning his parents. He was a handsome boy whose primary grade teachers considered him to be "cute" and "adorable" but "always in trouble." They complained about his poor work habits, distractability, and his need for attention. His third-grade teacher stated that he "stimulated the class to misbehavior." In the fourth grade he was reported to be "immature and playful, with no sense of responsibility." In the fifth grade he was described as a "truant" and a "bully" who threatened to beat children up if they crossed him or didn't do his bidding. Several of his teachers felt that his honesty could be questioned because he always seemed to know where missing articles could be found. His poor conduct and poor work habits persisted through the sixth grade where he was reading only at the 3.4 grade level. This type of behavior and poor achievement continued in the junior high school and he was retained in the eighth grade.

Another such child was Selma.

She was the third of five children in her family and was reported as an adjustment problem in the Washington School by each of her teachers in grades two to six. Yet Selma's classwork was good and she was conscientious and serious about monitorial responsibilities. Her teachers' comments present the best picture of her behavioral pattern.

Grade 1  "a nail biter and finger sucker. Constantly pushing and hitting children. Surprises me with her extensive knowledge."

Grade 2  "quite uninhibited. She is restless and fidgety, walks around the room at will, talks almost continuously, frequently interrupts when I am addressing the class."

Grade 3  "Sulks when she doesn't have her way. Children complain about her pushing and stepping on their feet when they are on line. She is easily angered when she is not called upon."

Grade 4  "She needs reassurance. She has a feeling of futility before any task, gives up before she starts. She is restless and talkative."

Grade 5  "She is constantly seeking attention. Her major problem is getting along with her classmates. She interferes verbally on any occasion and fights frequently. She is the butt of others as well, because she flares up so easily. She calls people names, mutters under her breath, and makes noises. She can be both sweet and horrible in the same day."

Her record in the sixth grade showed a continuation of this behavior and she was also given unsatisfactory ratings in self-control throughout her junior high school years.

There were other children who exhibited similar patterns of consistently aggressive behavior. One such boy, Ken, was born in Germany where his widowed mother met and subsequently married a black soldier. Another boy, Ted, who was reported four times, came from a family where parents, aunts, and uncles were teachers. He presented problems at home as well as in school, where even in the kindergarten, he sulked and struck other children. Here again, there was a continuation of this behavior, which gradually became aggravated into insolence to teachers and major disturbances in the school. This behavior persisted into junior and senior high school, from which he dropped out as soon as he could legally do so.

Aggressive behavior was also reported in the Jefferson School but it was of a somewhat different nature.

Peter, a handsome, dark-eyed, curly haired boy, with a Binet IQ of 121, was exuberant, gregarious, and very active even before he entered kindergarten. At the early registration session held in the spring it was reported that he ran in and out of the registration room, looking into classrooms, ignoring his mother's cautions. During the interview at that time his mother had revealed her concern over Peter's hyperactivity, strong will, and his demand for constant attention. It was also mentioned that he was an asthmatic child and had been "spoiled" by his parents. The behavior traits that were so evident from his first days of school, persisted throughout the grades and were a source of real annoyance to all of his teachers. Summaries of his behavior follow:

Kindergarten    "Peter is a very enthusiastic child. He likes to do everything but does not stay at any activity for too long a time. He does not follow orders if he doesn't wish to, but will go right on doing whatever he is doing even though he has been told to stop. If deprived of an activity for the day because he does not follow the rules, he will keep asking if he can go back to it. He is not affected by being reprimanded. He is a happy and sociable child and can be very helpful."

Grade 3    "He is a very mischievous child who sees humor in everything. He will do the deed and worry about consequences later. When consequences follow, he can't accept them. He would be very happy to be able to go along doing as he pleases without receiving punishment. He knows he will be punished, but cannot resist the prank. He can't function well in a group situation, cannot accept decisions of the group. He is motivated by attention-getting mechanisms. He will do anything to gain attention, whether ridiculous or heroic."

Grade 4    "In spite of all his annoying behavior, adults are very indulgent toward him because of his pleasing appearance, winning smile, and his ability to play on one's sympathy. He's a whiner, a pleader, a beggar—will promise anything for another chance. He never admits to a wrong and lies to save himself. Thinks he knows everything. A giggler—everything is a joke."

Peter explained his behavior in the following way to a teacher of another class on the grade, when she complained about his conduct in that room too:

"I don't mean to upset the class, I try my best but I goof. I think of funny cartoons and they make me laugh. I forget sad things but remember funny things. When I have an asthma attack I think I'll remember not to forget my hat because that made me sick but as soon as I'm better, I forget that. I say I'll never do it again, but then I do."

Grade 5    ". . . restless, unyielding, argumentative, on the defensive. Peter is aware of the fact that he causes frequent disturbances in the classroom as well as out of it. He seeks to justify his disorderly behavior, however, by attempting to argue his way out, pointing out that

others in the classroom are oftentimes at fault and are not reprimanded, explaining that he is the scapegoat by reorganizing incidents and facts in situations to suit his purposes. As a result of his
even greater rebellion after being reprimanded, he frequently evades
punishment."

Grade 6    His teacher found Peter's "heckling" very disturbing, and reported
that his behavior was boisterous and rude. This description of Peter's
behavior parallels the comments made by his teachers throughout
the junior high school years. In the seventh grade he was given a B
in Self-Control and the notation "Needs Improvement" appeared on
his record card next to the traits Cooperation, Courtesy, Social Participation, Effort. Although he received a "satisfactory" rating in
these traits in the eighth year, his ninth-grade teachers again recorded a need for improvement in these areas and he was given a C
in Self-Control.

In the high school, where only major infractions were reported, his tenth-grade
record had the following notations:

"Running on stairs—ordering lunch for another boy—threatened squad-
man"

"Disorder in prefect class"

"Smoking on school block" (Noted three times)

"Disturbing a class by knocking on window—probation"

Peter did not participate in any extracurricular activities in high school. His
grades were barely passable and he graduated with a general nonacademic
diploma. He was very much disappointed and when asked whether he was satisfied with his achievement in high school, he replied, "No, I have the potential
to do better than I did; I only got a general diploma."

Peter did not go to college but planned to "do outdoor work that's steady
and not too hard." In the ensuing few years he matured considerably and succeeded in becoming a policeman. He was quite satisfied with his work and
seemed to have made a satisfactory adjustment, until his death in the line of
duty at the age of twenty-three.

The only boy in the study who earned a double promotion was also
one who appeared quite consistently on lists of adjustment problems.

At an early age, William, one of the few black children in the Jefferson
School, began to show the results of his mother's ambitions and aspirations for
him. Kagan and Moss (1962, p. 204) state that "Theory and research have
acknowledged the profound importance of the mother as a determinant of the
child's behavior." This certainly was obvious in William's case. His mother con-
veyed to him her feeling that, because of his color, he was being discriminated
against by both pupils and teachers whenever he became involved in a behavioral difficulty. He was in the study in five grades and was reported as an adjustment problem in four of them. His second-grade teacher reported that he
was extremely sensitive and that he would begin to fight on the slightest provo-

cation. In the third grade when William's teacher complained to his mother about his uncontrollable temper when a child touched his toy or a book on his desk, his mother remarked, "He's an only child—he doesn't know how to play with others. At first I told him not to hit, but then I found it necessary for him to do so, and I taught him to defend himself."

William's difficulties in the fourth grade were created by his strong competitive drives. He was very bright, and usually the highest in achievement in all subjects, but when he didn't get the highest mark or when he was frustrated in any way, he would cry. He was an asthmatic child and any emotional upset would invariably be followed by an attack of asthma. Frequently, in his eagerness to be called upon to answer a question, he'd call out the answer before the teacher could call upon anyone. His parents were noticeably overprotective.

His fifth-grade teacher wrote in her summary: "Superior intellectual ability. High strung, nervous, suspicious. Has set extremely high standards for himself. Has a great deal of pressure from home. Is constantly comparing his work with others about him. He does not accept criticism easily, and feels that he's being picked on. Mother has come to school on several occasions to fight his battles."

His mother's rationalization perhaps can be seen from notations on his fifth-grade report card. Under Social Behavior his teacher had written: "William does not get along well with his classmates. I have to remind him not to call out and disturb his neighbors. He has been reported for talking while in line several times." The card was signed and returned with this comment written by William's mother: "It is amazing to me that such a prejudiced little girl (the monitor) has reported only *him* several times. I think too it would be well if you noticed the behavior of some of your so-called honor pupils instead of deliberately keeping your eyes glued to William." Any criticism of William by teachers or monitors was met with the accusation "you're picking on him," and each such experience was followed by his having an asthmatic attack which his mother called "emotional asthma."

Aware of William's excellent school grades, his mother began to pressure the principal into accelerating him. She came to school about this several times during the fifth grade and in March of that year, William, along with several other children, was advanced to the sixth grade. He and the others did very well academically and they were admitted to junior high school one year ahead of the rest of the study group. Even before classes started in junior high school, his mother pressured the school into placing William, already one year accelerated, into the Special Progress class. Again, though he did extremely well academically, and was the valedictorian at graduation from junior high school, his record showed that he had been referred to the guidance counselor several times because he did not get along with his peers in junior high school.

William admitted to the junior high school guidance counselor that he had had such difficulties in all grades of the elementary school with the exception of the few months he had spent in the sixth grade. The guidance counselor reported that he was "very competitive and could not acknowledge the fact that others could do better than him." William once told her, "If they do better it's because they're older than I." His mother came to school frequently, usually with a list of grievances showing how and where her son had been discriminated against because he was the only black boy in the class. His teachers said that she was really seeking preferential treatment and when this was not granted she considered it discrimination.

William did quite well in high school but his personality problems were not resolved. He was in several honors classes and was admitted to his high-school honor society. He responded to our questionnaire after graduation in which he was asked to evaluate himself. He thought his strong points were being "intelligent and very friendly," and his weakness was great sensitivity to criticism. However, when asked whether he was satisfied with his achievement in high school, he said, "Academically, I did very well. My only regret is that I didn't get to know more people."

William received a scholarship to an eastern college and was in his second year when we last heard from him.

Then there was Ella, a girl in the Jefferson School who exhibited different problems of behavior.

Play activities in the classroom and physical activities during the recess period were phases of school life that Ella seemed to dislike from the first grade, according to her anecdotal record. Her first-, second-, and third-grade teachers said that she had to be urged to participate in all activities, but especially physical ones. She was one of the children who had been listed as maladjusted because of her extreme shyness. Her first-grade teacher, however, considered her "advanced academically."

During an interview with her mother, in the third grade, it was revealed that Ella frequently asked her mother for notes to her teacher asking that she be excused from participating in gym activities. At times her mother would refuse to give her a note, but at other times she would give in to her and give her one. Mrs. B. seemed to feel that Ella was "afraid of losing."

In the fifth grade Ella was reported as being "extremely shy," but she was also listed as being "intellectually gifted." Her IQ on the Pintner-Cunningham Test given in the first grade was 145, and on the Otis Beta which she was given in the sixth grade, her IQ was 135. In an autobiography which she wrote in the fifth grade, she mentioned her shyness as something she didn't like about herself and also said, "Another thing that I dislike is that I'm not too active in gym. I'm always afraid of losing and if I do, I'm afraid that everyone will be mad at me." It was not an unusual sight to see Ella sitting on the sidelines in the sixth grade during the physical activities period. Those who did not bring their gym shoes were not allowed to participate in gym activities, and she frequently, and probably intentionally, left hers at home.

It is interesting, though not unexpected, to note that her shyness and fear of losing became apparent in other areas. In spite of the fact that Ella was academically one of the top achievers in each grade, she began to express a fear of tests in the fifth grade. In response to the question on a questionnaire *What makes you afraid?* she wrote, "Tests get me scared and nervous," and in the sixth grade, her responses to some open-ended statements were:

*I'm afraid when* "there's a test or problem to be solved and I doubt if I can do it right."

*I worry about* "my marks on tests. I'm always afraid of failing."

*The way I feel about school is* "I wish we didn't have it but as long as we do have it I like it pretty much."

*When I get to junior high school* "I would like special help in getting out of shyness."

That Ella's shyness was a source of concern for her mother was evident from conversations which she had had with teachers, the Project Assistant, and from responses to questions on parent questionnaires. Some of her answers follow:

Grade 1   *How has going to school helped your child?* "She is not as shy as she was before. At first she wouldn't participate in games in school or get up in front of the class to speak. She wouldn't voluntarily answer questions. She was helped to overcome these habits by a very thoughtful teacher."

Grade 3   *What qualities would you like her to develop further?* "To overcome her shyness."

Grade 6   *Is there anything about school that worries your child?* "Keeping her marks high."

*Do you think your child is satisfied with the progress she has made in elementary school?* "She always thinks she should have done better."

*What special interests does your child show outside of school?* "She doesn't seem to be interested in anything special. She dislikes doing anything new. I want her to learn to play an instrument. Although she likes to play the piano she hesitates."

Ella continued to do well in all her subjects in junior high school where she was in the accelerated Special Progress group. Most of her teachers, however, reported that she was shy, quiet, and that she rarely volunteered.

As we look back over these records which were gathered through the grades, it is perhaps easier to understand why early in the tenth grade in high school Ella developed school phobia. Insistence by the health education teacher upon her swimming in the school pool triggered several incidents. Ella had asked her doctor for a note excusing her from physical activity, but he refused because he felt it was good for her to participate in such activities. Soon Ella began finding school more and more difficult and a pattern of irregular attendance and daily complaints of nausea and dizziness began. The guidance counselor worked intensively with Ella, who had admitted to her that she was nervous in any new situation and also when reciting in class. Ella's academic performance was still excellent when she was able to attend school, and she achieved a 90% rating on a geometry test on her return to school after days of absence and apparent unhappiness.

Early in April of her first year (tenth grade) in high school, her difficulties became so severe that upon her doctor's advice, she was withdrawn from school. She was then getting regular psychiatric help, and was to return to high school the following September to repeat the tenth grade. Ella continued to receive psychiatric help when she returned and her tenth-grade teachers reported that she looked happy, participated, and that she was continuing to do well academically. However, in keeping with her basic difficulty, her average of 89.6% was not completely to her satisfaction.

Ella graduated from high school with good grades and went on to college. Her personality problems surfaced again and seriously affected her grades. She failed several subjects in her sophomore year and dropped out of college. Ella worked for a while in a business office and was subsequently married. She is now the mother of a young child.

It should not be concluded that seemingly well-adjusted children who were never reported did not have adjustment problems, sometimes of a serious nature.

Bess was always described by her teachers as a quiet, dependable, bright child with a strong sense of responsibility. She was well liked by her peers, and had been elected president of her class in the sixth grade. Yet in May of that school year she suddenly became fearful of tests, espcially in social studies, and she refused to go to school on days on which she expected tests. Soon nightmares were upsetting her, depression set in, and it became more and more difficult for her to go to school. At her doctor's suggestion her mother arranged an appointment with a neuropsychiatrist. By the middle of June after several weeks of medical help and with the cooperation of the school she was again attending school regularly, though she was still fearful of tests and was continuing with professional care. Just what happened to one of the best adjusted children in the study to cause these weeks of anxiety, we don't know.

As we look back, the only indications of Bess' concern about school were in her responses to questions on questionnaires which children answered in the fifth and sixth grades.

Grade 5  *What don't you like in school?* "I don't like social studies much."
Grade 6  *"I'm afraid when* "I get any kind of test." *I worry about* "all different kinds of tests."

Though Bess still visited the psychiatrist during the summer prior to her entrance to junior high school, she seemed to be much better and was attending school regularly when last heard from. Academically she was continuing to achieve well above average, consistent with her past record.

Perhaps the most dramatic conclusion of our study of adjustment is found not in the tables nor in related data, but in an examination of behavior patterns. In a study at the Fels Institute, Kagan and Moss

(1962) document the remarkable continuity in behavior displayed from age 10 through early adulthood. The very same may be said of the consistency of behavior shown by the children in the study from kindergarten through their junior high school years. It is a sobering thought to realize that in spite of the combined efforts, over a 10-year period, of school personnel and sometimes in spite of psychiatric help, the behavior of many of the children with problems could have been predicted in the primary grades.

Let us isolate comments about Stewart, with an IQ of 138, made by a dozen teachers in the elementary and junior high schools which he attended, in which faculties did not know one another and had no access to our records.

### CLASS PARTICIPATION

Grade 2   "Objects to carrying out certain assignments."
Grade 4   "He rarely will finish his written work."
Grade 6   "Evades work and responsibility."
Grade 7   "Does no work" (Reported by teachers of Spanish, Science, Typing).
Grade 9   "If he happens to take a fancy to work, he'll do it. If not, he'll stare into space. Gives up too easily. Rarely finishes."

### BEHAVIOR AND ATTITUDES

Kindergarten   "Looks sad, refuses to participate."
Grade 2   "Sulky—puzzling, hard to reach."
Grade 4   "Rather removed, aloof, moody, rarely smiles."
          "I always have the feeling that Stewart is capable of violent and antisocial responses—like a volcano waiting to erupt."
Grade 5   "Sullen, morose, seldom smiles or laughs. Gives one the feeling that he is constantly inhibiting his emotions."
Grade 8   "Some day you're going to read about Stewart. His emotions are all bottled up."
Grade 9   "His serious look is moody rather than mature. He doesn't express emotion."
          "He's quiet in class, but I'm waiting for some sort of explosion."
          "He's going to explode someday, there will be headlines about him."

Stewart went on to high school where his work and behavior were consistently poor and he left school without graduating. There followed a series of odd jobs and then service in the army from which he received a dishonorable discharge. Brushes with the law became frequent until he was finally convicted for the sale and possession of drugs.

This case supports the conclusions of a study by Westman, Rice, and Bermann, who write:

The evidence . . . contradicts the time-honored notion that children out-grow behavior problems seen in early life and supports the thesis that drastic shifts in manifest behavior tend not to occur in the first 18 years of life . . . It is clear . . . that, in general, problems identified early are harbingers of later problems [1967, p. 728].

Consider the comments about Helene:

Grade 1   "Doesn't speak to anyone."
Grade 2   "On fringe of class throughout class discussions."
Grade 3   "Always quiet, alone."
Grade 7   "Exceptionally quiet, doesn't relate to other children, so withdrawn."
Grade 8   "Quiet, shy, alone."
Grade 9   "She is all alone, not disliked by children, but she doesn't seek them out."

Helene managed to get along fairly well in high school and completed a commercial course.

It should be reemphasized that among the many needs of our schools is a greatly expanded program of guidance and psychiatric assistance which must function along with the instructional program beginning in the kindergarten. Stennett contends that a "significant number of children identified as emotionally handicapped are not likely to resolve their adjustment problems without help" (1966, p. 449). Although there is no way of knowing whether and at what point such help might have been most efficient in altering patterns of behavior, it seems clear that the availability of special services only for emergencies precludes the possibility of establishing a long-range preventive and treatment program.

It should also be pointed out that the need is as great in so-called "advantaged" schools as it is in schools in underprivileged areas. As has been shown in Chapter Four, the few children in the Jefferson School who were able to get private remedial and/or psychiatric help made great strides in their achievement as well as in their general adjustment. It must be concluded that if it is the purpose of the school to upset predictions, then we have failed in our purpose.

### CHILDREN WHO WERE HURT

Another question this project was designed to investigate pertains to the effect of traumatic experiences upon children's learning and adjustment. The problem of defining "traumatic" is not a simple one. What is traumatic for one person may not be traumatic for another; what is shattering for one child may leave another apparently unscathed.

In selecting for study children who may have been traumatized, the criteria for identifying a traumatic experience were those which the literature in this field generally accepts. For our purposes, the impact of the experience was thought to be of greater importance than its nature. For example, the death of a parent who had been severely ill for a long time was considered to be less traumatic than the sudden death of a parent. As has been mentioned in Chapter Two, a child who has been exposed to constant discord between parents may find relief rather than trauma when the parents are divorced. On the other hand, a child who is shielded from parental disagreements may find the announcement of a divorce exceedingly shattering. Selected for examination here are the cases of those children whose experiences most people would judge to be traumatic and where the project staff, on the basis of their knowledge of the total situation, were in agreement.

Consider, then, the cases of the following children:

Edward came from a family with very high academic motivation and standards which were, in general, matched by the achievement of its members. One of his sisters is a teacher, another did very well at one of the specialized high schools, and an older brother whom Edward worshipped had been awarded a scholarship to study piano at a conservatory in Paris. After his return to the United States Edward's brother gave several concerts and subsequently obtained a position with an advertising agency, where he wrote music for TV commercials.

When Edward was interviewed in the second grade, he answered the question "What do you wish you were?" by saying, "I wish I were a musician like my brother." This affection for and idolization of his brother continued throughout the elementary grades. In drawing a picture of his family, Edward always drew his brother first. In response to the assignment "Draw a picture of a person," Edward drew a picture and labeled it, "My Brother."

Edward was rated average or better than average on all scales and his achievement was always above grade level.

In the fourth grade Edward's teacher asked the class to write on the theme "My Happiest Day." Edward wrote

"My happiest day was when my mother came home with my brother. My brother almost died from an accident in Ottawa. And he came back on a train."

It was only then that we learned that during the previous summer, Edward's brother had married, and on a honeymoon trip had been involved in a severe accident in which his bride was killed and which hospitalized him for several months. When questioned, Edward spoke of his brother glowingly, "My brother came out of the hospital. He's home now. He's teaching me how to play the piano and gives me a lesson every Sunday." A few weeks later, Edward's teacher was absent because of the death of her grandfather. When she returned she found the following note on her desk:

Dear Mrs. ———,
    We know what happened from the principal. I know how you feel from when they called us from Canada about my brother. You still have yourself to think of so don't worry and come back soon.
Sincerely yours,<br>Edward

It would probably be generally agreed that Edward's experience was both profound and traumatic. There is no way of measuring the depth of the impact and the variety of effects upon him. If we restrict ourselves to an examination of his work in school and of his ratings on the adjustment scale, we find no noticeable change in the quality of his work, scores on his achievement tests, or in his general adjustment during the entire period. As was indicated previously, neither teacher nor Project Assistant was even aware of the anguish and concern that Edward must have suffered immediately after the accident and during the many months that his brother had been hospitalized away from home. Edward completed high school and college where his achievement was consistently above average. He now holds a responsible position in the computer industry.

And then there was Susan:

Susan with an IQ of 90 was considered of average mentality and achieved accordingly. She was usually immaculately dressed, well groomed, and her walk had a gay lilt to it.

What Susan lacked in intellectual superiority, she more than made up for in what was considered a vivid imagination. In periods devoted to oral expression she was eager to entertain the class with her imaginative experiences and with details of cooking potatoes and drinking Pepsi-Cola for breakfast. One Monday morning in her second-grade class, during a so-called "Show and Tell" period, one of the children who lived in the same building as Susan began telling of a disturbance in their apartment house over the weekend in which Susan's mother had been shot. The teacher stopped the narration and then went on to more educationally promising activities. Nothing more was said of

**Table 6-7  Children with Traumatic Experiences**

| | Nature of Experience | Grade | IQ Test [a] | IQ Score | Reading Grade Score 1 [b] | 2 | 3 | 4 | 5 | 6 | Adjustment Scale 1 | 2 | 3 | 4 | 5 | 6 |
|---|---|---|---|---|---|---|---|---|---|---|---|---|---|---|---|---|
| | | | | | *Jefferson School* | | | | | | | | | | | |
| **Boys** | | | | | | | | | | | | | | | | |
| W.J. | Retarded brother institution | 2 | PC | 144 | 90 | 3.5 | 4.7 | 5.9 | 6.2 | 7.2 | 1 | | 3 [c] | 1 | 2 | 5 |
| | | | Alpha | 119 | | | | | | | | | | | | |
| | | | Beta | 124 | | | | | | | | | | | | |
| P.J. | Parents separated | 4 | PC | 112 | 80 | 2.4 | 3.9 | 4.5 | 8.5 | 6.5 | 1 | 2 | 1 | 2 | 2 | 2 |
| | | | Alpha | 93 | | | | | | | | | | | | |
| | | | Beta | 112 | | | | | | | | | | | | |
| D.S. | Court fight re custody | 4 | PC | 145 | — | — | 4.8 | 6.6 | 7.2 | 8.8 | — | — | | 3 | 3 | 3 |
| | | | Alpha | 131 | | | | | | | | | | | | |
| | | | Beta | 139 | | | | | | | | | | | | |
| **Girls** | | | | | | | | | | | | | | | | |
| V.L. | Separated parents | 3 | PC | 122 | 90 | 2.4 | 2.5 | 3.4 | 4.2 | 4.4 | 2 | 3 | 2 | 2 | 4 | 2 |
| | | | Alpha | 99 | | | | | | | | | | | | |
| | | | Beta | 93 | | | | | | | | | | | | |
| H.M. | Mother's death | 4 | PC | 114 | 10 | 3.7 | 4.6 | 6.2 | 8.4 | 8.1 | 2 | 4 | 1 | 2 | 2 | 3 |
| | | | Alpha | 101 | | | | | | | | | | | | |
| | | | Beta | 125 | | | | | | | | | | | | |

| Subject | Event | Grade | IQ (PC / Alpha / Beta)[a] | %ile[b] | Reading scores | | | | | Ratings[c] | | | | | |
|---|---|---|---|---|---|---|---|---|---|---|---|---|---|---|---|
| M.H. | Brother severe polio | 3 | PC 96, Alpha 92, Beta 100 | 10 | 2.7 | 3.3 | 3.8 | 5.5 | 5.7 | 4 | 1 | 3 | 2 | 2 | 1 |

### Washington School

| Subject | Event | Grade | IQ (PC / Alpha / Beta)[a] | %ile[b] | Reading scores | | | | | Ratings[c] | | | | | |
|---|---|---|---|---|---|---|---|---|---|---|---|---|---|---|---|
| **Boys** | | | | | | | | | | | | | | | |
| B.J. | Mother's death | 2 | PC 116, Alpha 99, Beta 95 | 70 | 2.5 | 3.8 | 4.8 | 5.8 | 5.6 | 1 | 1 | 2 | 3 | 4 | 2 |
| M.V. | Divorce | 3 | PC 99, Alpha 103, Beta 96 | 40 | 2.9 | 3.2 | 4.7 | 4.9 | 6.3 | — | 4 | 4 | 5 | 5 | 2 |
| E.M. | Brother injured | 4 | PC 115, Alpha 108, Beta 104 | 60 | 2.9 | 3.3 | 4.3 | 6.7 | 6.9 | 1 | 3 | 1 | 2 | 1 | 1 |
| **Girls** | | | | | | | | | | | | | | | |
| S.Y. | Mother shot | 3 | PC 90 | 10 | 2.2 | — | — | — | — | 2 | 3 | 1 | — | — | — |

*Note:* Scores and ratings after incident follow solid lines.

[a] PC = Pintner-Cunningham Primary Test; Alpha, Beta = forms of Otis Quick-Scoring Mental Ability Tests.

[b] Percentile Score.

[c] Rating of 1 = very well adjusted; rating of 5 = very poorly adjusted.

the incident and Susan continued to function in her usual way. At the end of the second grade, she obtained a reading score which was approximately normal and she was considered fairly well adjusted on the adjustment scale. Shortly after the beginning of the third grade an officer of the Society for the Prevention of Cruelty to Children came to the school and informed the principal that Susan's mother had attempted suicide and that Susan was to be transferred to a home for neglected children. It was only then that the Project Assistant in speaking to Susan, referred to the shooting incident which Susan described as follows:

> My uncle came to visit my mother and they had an argument, and he shot her. I was hiding under the bed. They took my mother to the hospital and it was only a flesh wound so she came home the next day.

During her brief time in the third grade, her teacher considered her to be very well adjusted. Here again, as far as could be observed, the experience had no observable effect upon her learning or school adjustment.

Consider the case of Daniel:

Daniel's parents had been divorced and after his father had remarried, Daniel lived with his father and stepmother. His maternal grandmother had visiting privileges and spent one day each week with him. On one of these visits, Daniel complained to his grandmother that he had been beaten by his father and showed her some bruises which had allegedly been inflicted. His grandmother immediately took Daniel to his mother, who resided in another state. Following an alarm that was broadcast through regular police channels for both grandmother and child, they returned to New York along with his mother, who appealed to the Court for a reconsideration of Daniel's custody. At this second hearing, which Daniel also attended, the Court again awarded custody to his father and ordered that the child be sent back to him. He returned to school on a day that a standardized reading test was given and achieved one of the highest scores in the class, consistent with his superior IQ.

Daniel's superior performance continued and he was reported by his teacher to be well adjusted and "happy." Adjustment with his stepmother also seemed to be good.

There were other cases. There was Walter, whose younger brother was placed in a mental institution for the retarded and who himself underwent surgery for cancer. And there were Paul, Vera, and Matthew, whose parents were separated or divorced; there was Hazel, whose mother died shortly after childbirth leaving her and her father and brother with a one-week-old baby. Data for these children are shown in Table 6-7.

In assessing the impact of these incidents and experiences on our children, we can only conclude that in no case did any one traumatic experience have any apparent effect upon learning or adjustment as viewed by teachers and the project staff. We can only conjecture how much of the hurt, if any, was internalized and what effect it may subsequently have on these children. With the exception of Susan, all of the children remained with us for a period of at least three years following the experience, and in no case can it definitely be said that a change in pattern resulted.

It may be that children like Susan, in self-defense, encase themselves in shatterproof tombs in which nothing touches them and from which no emotions emanate. Such children learn early in life that to be touched or to react is painful.

We may be seeing in Susan the cumulative effects of neglect, deprivation, and rejection. Jersild notes that "under conditions of severe rejection, a child is like a warrior who is wounded even before he has a chance to fight" (1968, p. 203). Susan entered the kindergarten already "wounded," an illegitimate child of a prostitute. In retrospect, we can only marvel at her strengths and inner resources which enabled her to function adequately in the classroom, to establish good and sometimes affectionate relationships with her teachers, to learn, and to escape the crippling anger and hostility so common to severely traumatized children.

Our children seemed to show the resiliency peculiar to most children, and they managed to react to their environment adequately while coping with their own special problems.

## THE FEARFUL ONES

What supervisor and teacher has not watched the excitement and the anticipation of newly enrolled kindergarten children filing into the playground or into their classrooms on the opening day of school to begin the great adventure of formal education? Suddenly their world expands and becomes more complex. What are children's thoughts and how do they feel when they leave the comparative safety and security of their homes and come into a playground or auditorium with hundreds of children, or even into a classroom of 30 or 40 children? This we don't know, but we do know that it may be overwhelming to some, whereas others seem to take it in their stride. The retrospection of older children or adults concerning their first day in school is helpful, but it does not give us a qualitative or accurate picture of the impact of the experience.

We know that some children come eagerly, wave farewells to their parents, take their places in line or go into the classrooms excited with the promise of each new experience, and accept the leadership of the teacher. We know that others do it hesitatingly and show visible signs of anxiety. And then, there are always children who must be urged and coaxed and reassured, as they leave their parents tearfully or cling to them and insist that they remain in the room with them.

When our children entered the kindergarten we saw examples of each of these types. During the registration period of the previous spring, many children had already exhibited the behavior they were to show. Thus, when school opened in September, particular attention was paid to those children who seemed fearful or who were having difficulty leaving their mothers.

In speaking of these children, we are referring to them as showing problems of separation rather than those of school phobia. Sarason et al. point out, "In the case of the school phobic child who is starting school for the first time, one wonders how appropriate it is to talk of a school phobia. It is the act of separation rather than the idea of school which is the immediate antecedent of the reaction" (1960, p. 26). Kaplan (1965) contends that this fear of being separated is frequently fostered unconsciously by some mothers, who maintain their children in a state of dependency to satisfy their own needs.

No two children were exactly alike in the way they showed their anxiety, nor were the reactions of their mothers alike. A few mothers were noticeably annoyed, almost all were embarrassed, and many showed obvious stress and anxiety. One mother verbalized her concern by saying, "If this is the picture on the first morning of school, what can I expect later on?"

Before the opening day of school, it was suggested to principals and teachers that they permit mothers to remain in kindergarten classrooms until such time as children were able to have them leave. School personnel were exceedingly cooperative and contributed immensely in helping children to adjust to the school situation.

In attempting to identify children who were having separation problems the following criteria of behavior were selected:

Unwillingness to enter the room.
Insisting upon mother being within sight.
Crying, clinging, or soiling at any time during the first three weeks.

It should be recognized here that there are certain limitations in our methods of identifying children who were having separation problems. For one thing, we were identifying only those children who felt free to express their anxiety. This, in itself, was indicative of a healthier personality and probably warranted a prediction of subsequent early adjustment.

Second, we have no way of knowing how children had been prepared for their entrance to school and how many parents had urged, coaxed, bribed, or threatened their children to show no fear and not to cry. For example, a teacher recalled that in a previous year, she had seen one mother literally dragging her crying daughter down the hall saying, "Now you get into the classroom and keep quiet," and so the child went into the classroom and kept quiet. We never knew how many children internalized their anxiety, either repressing it completely or exhibiting it in other unrelated ways.

What were these children like who so overtly exhibited their anxiety? In discussing them we are including all children who showed separation problems whether or not they remained to become part of our basic population. Tables 6-8 and 6-9 summarize a variety of data for them.

As can be seen from the tables, the children who showed separation anxiety were representative of the entire population of their grades. The means of their subsequent scores on intelligence tests and reading readiness tests approximated the means for their class. Some apparent deterioration in performance and seemingly significant variation from the class means is due not to the fact that the group happened to include some children who later developed serious reading problems, but rather to the coincidence whereby a number of children with superior IQ scores moved away from each of the schools. The original group were certainly not the dullest children; neither, however, were all these children the brightest, although their kindergarten teachers considered them above average. The group in both schools included some who were to become our most mature and well-adjusted pupils, as well as those who were destined to be consistently identified as adjustment problems. Here, also, were those who became very successful in school and those who failed.

Ordinal positions in the family did not seem to differ from those of the larger group of children who showed no difficulty in entering school. No conclusions can be drawn from the fact that there were many more first and only children in the Jefferson School than in the Washington School. This was characteristic of the entire Jefferson School population. It will be recalled that this school adjoined a new low middle-income housing project where the small apartments attracted young parents with few children.

It is interesting to examine the retrospective reports of our children. When we asked them in the second grade, "Remember when you first started school? How did you feel?", more than half of those who had shown separation anxiety had no memory of their difficulties and recalled positive feelings such as, "happy," "glad." When we asked them the same

Table 6-8 Children With Separation Problems—Adjustment and Achievement—Jefferson School

| | Ordinal Position in Family | Reported as Adjustment Problem (K 1 2 3 4 5 6) | Adjustment Scale Rating [a] (1 2 3 4 5 6) | IQ Pintner-Cunningham (1) | IQ Otis Alpha (3) | IQ Otis Beta (6) | NYRR [b] Percentile (1) | Reading Metropolitan [c] Grade Score (3) | Reading Metropolitan [c] Grade Score (6) | Mathematics Metropolitan [c] Grade Score (6) |
|---|---|---|---|---|---|---|---|---|---|---|
| **Boys** | | | | | | | | | | |
| G.G. | Only | x x x x x x x | 4 5 4 5 4 4 | 101 | 99 | 103 | 30 | 2.3 | 4.8 | 5.9 |
| S.B. | 2 | x x x  x x x | 5 3 4 5 5 4 | 93 | 86 | 75 | 40 | 2.1 | 3.5 | 6.6 |
| S.I. | 1 | x x x x   x | 1 3 4 2 2 5 | 106 | 101 | 101 | 70 | 4.5 | 8.1 | 6.1 |
| S.S. | 1 | | 1 2 1 1 1 1 | 115 | 90 | 132 | 90 | 4.7 | 9.4 | 10+ |
| W.D. | 1 | | 1 1 1 1 1 1 | 110 | 88 | 120 | 90 | 4.1 | 7.8 | 8.0 |
| S.L. | 2 | Discharged grade 2 | 1 – – – – – | 123 | – | – | 80 | – | – | – |
| B.N. | 1 | Discharged grade 2 | 1 – – – – – | 139 | – | – | 90 | – | – | – |
| B.E. | 1 | Discharged grade 2 | 3 – – – – – | 101 | – | – | 80 | – | – | – |
| B.J. | 1 | Discharged grade 4 | 1 1 1 – – – | 140 | 118 | – | 90 | 5.3 | – | – |
| **Girls** | | | | | | | | | | |
| H.A. | Only | x x x | 3 3 1 4 4 3 | 82 | 79 | 91 | 10 | 3.1 | 5.0 | 6.3 |
| W.A. | 1 | Discharged grade 5 | 2 2 1 2 – – | 100 | 92 | – | 80 | 2.8 | – | – |
| R.C. | 1 | Discharged grade 3 | 3 3 2 – – – | 143 | – | – | 80 | – | – | – |
| Mean | | | | 112.8 | 94.1 | 103.6 | 69.2 | 3.6 | 6.4 | 7.2 |
| Total class mean | | | | 112.5 | 104.0 | 112.5 | 71.8 | 4.0 | 7.4 | 7.9 |

[a] Rating of 1 = very well adjusted; rating of 5 = very poorly adjusted.

[b] New York Reading Readiness Test.

[c] Metropolitan Reading or Mathematics Test—Primary, Elementary, Intermediate—as appropriate to the grade level.

**Table 6-9  Children With Separation Problems—Adjustment and Achievement—Washington School**

| Grade: | Ordinal Position in Family — K | Reported as Adjustment Problem (K 1 2 3 4 5 6) | Adjustment Scale Rating[a] (1) | (2) | (3) | (4) | (5) | (6) | IQ Pintner-Cunningham (1) | Otis Alpha (3) | Otis Beta (6) | NYRR[b] Percentile (1) | Reading Metropolitan[c] Grade Score (3) | (6) | Mathematics Metropolitan[c] Grade Score (6) |
|---|---|---|---|---|---|---|---|---|---|---|---|---|---|---|---|
| **Boys** | | | | | | | | | | | | | | | |
| C.L. | 2 | Discharged and readmitted  x  x x | – | 3 | 2 | 2 | – | 5 | 96 | – | 81 | – | – | 4.3 | 3.7 |
| B.C. | 2 | Discharged grade 4  x x x | 3 | 3 | 2 | – | – | – | 117 | – | – | 80 | – | – | – |
| H.T. | 2 | Discharged grade 3  x x x | 1 | 2 | – | – | – | – | 101 | – | – | 10 | – | – | – |
| **Girls** | | | | | | | | | | | | | | | |
| M.J. | 1 | x x x x | 1 | 4 | 5 | 2 | 3 | 4 | 94 | 80 | 95 | 0 | 2.3 | 3.5 | 3.6 |
| W.V. | 2 | x   x | 1 | 3 | 3 | 2 | 3 | 4 | 78 | 89 | 86 | 10 | 3.9 | 3.6 | 3.9 |
| P.R. | 3 | | 1 | 1 | 1 | 1 | 1 | 1 | 94 | 106 | 101 | 60 | 3.9 | 6.2 | 6.0 |
| R.M. | 2 | | 1 | 1 | 2 | 1 | 2 | 2 | 119 | 108 | 107 | 80 | 4.5 | 7.7 | 9.4 |
| B.D. | Only | | 1 | 1 | 1 | 1 | 2 | 1 | 103 | 87 | 99 | 90 | 3.3 | 7.0 | 6.8 |
| H.L. | 2 | | 1 | 2 | 1 | 2 | 1 | 2 | 118 | 90 | 115 | 70 | 4.3 | 7.6 | 10.5 |
| S.V. | 2 | Discharged grade 4 | 1 | 1 | 1 | – | – | – | 100 | 97 | – | 50 | 3.8 | – | – |
| C.R. | 2 | Discharged grade 3 | 1 | 1 | – | – | – | – | 107 | – | – | 70 | – | – | – |
| Mean | | | | | | | | | 102.5 | 93.9 | 97.7 | 52.0 | 3.7 | 5.7 | 6.3 |
| Total class mean | | | | | | | | | 98.6 | 95.8 | 97.3 | 54.6 | 3.5 | 6.0 | 6.6 |

[a] Rating of 1 = very well adjusted; rating of 5 = very poorly adjusted.
[b] New York Reading Readiness Test.
[c] Metropolitan Reading or Mathematics Test—Primary, Elementary, Intermediate—as appropriate to the grade level.

101

question in grades five and six, all but one recalled that they had really been "scared," "worried," "afraid." On the other hand, most of our other children who had exhibited no separation problems upon admission to school gave almost identical answers in the second grade—"happy," "glad"—and again in the fifth and sixth grades also recalled being "scared" and "afraid." The same question was asked again upon their graduation from high school, 13 years after the experience. Of the 64 who responded, 17 could not remember that first day, including one girl who had separation problems; 19 remembered only positive, pleasant experiences; and 28, including only one who had problems, remembered being "scared" or "nervous." Typical of their comments was this statement:

> On that first day I remember trying to be brave in front of all the other children. I said good-bye to my mother while some children cried. I was really very scared but I didn't want anyone to know it.

In questionnaires given to parents of children in the first, third, and sixth grades, there was no distinction between the responses of parents of the anxious and nonanxious children to the questions, "Does he like school?" (to which almost all answers were positive), "Is he a problem at home?" and "Is there anything about school that worries him?" The separation-anxiety children in the Washington School did, however, differ from children in the Jefferson School in that more of them remembered their early anxiety when questioned in the second grade, as well as in the fifth and sixth.

Let us now look at some of the children who exhibited severe anxiety.

Paula, a shy child, sat quietly playing with a puzzle while her mother was being interviewed in the spring prior to her entrance to kindergarten. Her mother had indicated that she was eager to go to school because her sister and brother were attending school and she wanted to go, too. On the first day of school, however, Paula screamed for about 15 minutes, and her mother remained in the room until she had calmed down and stopped crying. The next day, the child again cried but her mother did not stay. Paula's teacher, who had had her brother and sister in previous classes, talked to Paula, saying, "Your sister was in this room when she first came to school; your brother was in this room, too. And now you're here."

Talking to Paula and getting her involved with something to do seemed to help the situation. She no longer cried, but for the first two weeks Paula was mostly an onlooker, though she was friendly and warm toward her teacher. New experiences or changes in routine did not seem to upset her. Soon, she was relating well to the children, began to smile freely, and played happily, though at times she seemed withdrawn. In March of this kindergarten year, it was reported that Paula's father, who had been hospitalized for a long time, had died.

Her teacher reported that there seemed to be no obvious change in Paula's behavior.

Throughout the six years of school that followed, Paula was rated 1, very well adjusted, by all her teachers. On sociometric measures, Paula did very well, being among the most chosen in all grades. In the third grade she was singled out by her teacher as being socially gifted and was chosen president of the class by the children. Evaluations by her teachers in the fourth, fifth, and sixth grades were very much in agreement. They considered her quiet, neat, a good worker, interested and capable. One teacher said, "She's quiet, but stands up for her rights in a dignified way."

In the fifth and sixth grades, Paula recalled her initial anxiety when answering the question, "How did you feel when you first started school?" When asked the same question in the second grade, however, her response had been, "I felt all right. Everybody was nice to me."

Of average intelligence, Paula was at grade level in academic standing at the end of the sixth grade and continued to perform satisfactorily through the junior and senior high school.

Consider the case of Helene, who was discussed briefly as an adjustment problem:

Helene, an only child, entered kindergarten after having had a visit the previous spring. At the time, she seemed to be enthusiastic about her visit and had asked to stay longer. On the first day of school, however, Helene cried violently, clung to her mother, who remained in the room for the full session. During the remainder of the first week she cried as soon as her mother attempted to leave and so her mother stayed. She played but often looked at her mother and went to her for approval of her work. Her mother was eager to cooperate and directed Helene to the teacher for any assistance while she kept herself occupied in the room, occasionally helping the kindergarten group. She was willing to remain as long as was necessary.

During the first two weeks Helene had practically no contact with the other children and sat by herself most of the time. Since she always went to her mother for advice, she had almost no relationship with the teacher, either. She spent her time playing with beads, pegs, or crayons, and was very apprehensive and insecure about new experiences or changes in routines. The presence of her mother seemed to be imperative.

Toward the end of the second week, although Helene still wanted her mother to stay, her play became more relaxed, and she was willing to allow her mother to sit outside the classroom, saying to her teacher, "My mommy will wait outside."

At the end of this acute three-week period, Helene was more social and related better to most of the children. She also communicated more freely with her teacher and was more friendly toward her. At times, when the teacher left the room, Helene would ask where she was going. She was anxious but accepted new experiences more readily. There was now a noticeably better adjustment to school. Her mother needed no longer to remain in school, and sometimes Helene came to school with a neighbor.

After about six months had passed, Helene felt free with the children, but had made no special attachments, and so worked alone for a large part of the time. She was close to the teacher, and went to her for praise, help, and encouragement, all of which were willingly given. Though she had an exploratory interest in all materials, she still needed reassurance with new experiences and with changes in routines, but she seemed to have greater confidence in herself.

At the end of the kindergarten year, her teacher reported, "Helene has improved considerably since the beginning of the term. She is interested in many activities in school. Her attention span is long when she is doing something she likes. She is immature in her approach to coloring, painting, pasting, woodwork and puzzles. She plays well with the children and has a good sense of right and wrong. She often helps children clean up and corrects them when they make a mistake."

The handling that seemed to help Helene was the patient cooperation of her mother and the calm, firm, friendly, and patient attitude of her first teacher. Commending those children who allowed their parents to go home and praising Helene when she allowed her mother to remain outside of the room also may have helped.

In the following year in the first grade, there was no evidence of any first-day difficulties. Most observations of Helene noted her serious, intent attitude and slow pace. Her mother now began to show concern about her child's achievement and lack of friends. Though the Pintner-Cunningham Test showed her to be of low normal intelligence, Helene read words well, but with little understanding. She spoke in a husky voice with little variety of tonal expression. In classroom socialization, she usually was on the fringe of the group. This pattern persisted throughout the elementary grades and the junior high school.

In the fourth and fifth grades, Helene's hearing was checked but a medical examination showed that there was no hearing defect. Her fifth-grade teacher reported, "Helene doesn't answer when asked a question—as though she hasn't heard it." Her sixth-grade teacher reported that she had never seen Helene talking to another child, nor had she seen any children speaking to her, and that Helene spoke only when spoken to. Her mother stated that the director of the camp which Helene had attended the previous summer also reported that Helene did not participate, did not make friends. Mrs. A. decided that it might be advisable for her to get outside professional help with Helene, and she therefore applied to a community agency.

During the seventh grade of junior high school the family was being seen at a treatment center, and Helene had begun receiving private instruction in reading. Her tutor said that she knew the mechanics of reading, but that her comprehension and vocabulary were very poor, and that she required a good deal of help. In the eighth grade, Helene received help from an agency because her tutor had given up private work. Most teachers in the junior high school considered her to be "exceptionally quiet, withdrawn, alone." Her eighth-grade teacher of science remarked, "Helene talks only to the girl next to her, and because it isn't really disturbing, and because she is otherwise so quiet, I allow it." And another teacher said, "She is all alone; she's not disliked by the children, but she doesn't seek them out, and they don't seek her."

Helene was graduated from junior high school, having passed all her subjects. On the ninth-grade reading test, she achieved a grade score of 7.5 in spite of the fact that she had been receiving help with her reading throughout the junior high school grades.

Helene did quite well in high school, especially in commercial subjects. She volunteered her services as secretary to several teachers and departmental offices in her school, and she seemingly made a very satisfactory adjustment. Her high school record also shows that she served as a hospital volunteer for the American Red Cross and she won an award for excellence in Bookkeeping upon graduation.

Another interesting example is Wayne.

Wayne, a good looking boy with large, sparkling black eyes, showed separation anxiety from the day of registration by refusing to enter the room. He repeated over and over, "I'll go to school in the winter," as his mother tried to get him to enter the room on a spring registration day. In describing him his mother said that he was shy, that he followed her around at all times. She mentioned, too, that Wayne was able to dress himself and help dress the two younger children, and that he was just beginning to play alone on the sidewalk in front of his apartment building.

On the first day of school, Wayne cried and fearfully clung to his mother as they walked through the hallway to the kindergarten room. His mother, teary-eyed, distraught, and embarrassed, remained in the room for the full session. Wayne sat close to her and she accompanied him when he went to select a game or moved to another part of the room. On the second day, though his mother stayed close by, Wayne followed instructions from his teacher. He was absent for the three remaining days of that first week, and when he returned the second week, his mother again remained in the classroom. Wayne participated in the class program only when the activities were such that they would allow his mother to sit near him. The situation was the same for the third week, but during the fourth and fifth weeks there were some signs of improvement. He was now willing to leave his mother's side, but he would turn frequently to see if she was still there. For a few days his mother sat in the hall, while Wayne sat inside the room near the door, peeping out frequently.

One day during the sixth week of the term, his mother escorted Wayne to the classroom and told him that she was going home because she had a cold. He cried, clung to her, said he wanted to stay in school, but he wanted her to stay outside the room. Finally, after 15 minutes of crying, he was taken home. The next day, two neighbors brought him in, one promising to stay a few minutes. When she left, Wayne put his head in his teacher's lap and cried, "I want my mommy. I want to go home." He cried for about 10 minutes, then stretched out on the floor and fell sound asleep. A few days later when he was again brought in by a neighbor, he came right into the room, sat with the children, poked the boy next to him, touched the blocks on the shelf near him, giggled a great deal, played the piano when he thought no one would notice him doing it, and acted as though this had been normal behavior for him.

For the first six weeks of the term Wayne had been an onlooker rather than a participant. But after that, he attached himself to a different child each day. He accepted help from the teacher, but rarely asked for it. However, after this acute stage was over, Wayne participated freely in most activities. His mother was now no longer needed in school. He was particularly good at working out puzzles, handling blocks, using clay and paints, and he seemed to enjoy everything. He showed excellent motor ability and coordination. When the children were asked to draw pictures of their families, he refused to do one. Though he had had severe tantrums at the beginning of the year, there were none now. However, after an absence from school, he would frequently become sullen and withdrawn.

Now, as the term progressed, Wayne seemed happy and usually had a big smile. He enjoyed active play but was also able to concentrate on seat work for a long period of time. He was generally independent, tried to get along without coming to an adult for help, but observed adults intently. After his initial difficulties he responded well to other children, helped them with materials, instigated giggling, and talked a great deal. At the end of the kindergarten year his teacher reported, "Although we had a great deal of difficulty getting Wayne to stay in class without his mother, Wayne is now one of the best adjusted children. He works and plays well with others, is cooperative, and has an excellent speaking vocabulary."

When, in the following year, Wayne started the first grade, he showed no hesitancy in coming to school, and he became an active member of the class almost at once. At an interview with his mother which took place early in the first grade, she said that Wayne loved school, went to bed early each night in happy anticipation of school the next day, and that he showed no anxiety about leaving home. He was one of the "most chosen" children on a sociogram done in class in which children were asked "Whom would you like to sit next to?" Throughout the grades he was among the most popular of children. His adjustment rating was 1, the highest, in the first grade and in all subsequent grades, and he was rated Enthusiastic in class activity in all grades but one, when he was rated Interested. He did well in reading, and his teacher thought he was extremely bright though his Pintner-Cunningham IQ was only 110. In all grades he made good progress in reading and he was considered to have marked interest in it.

Wayne was an active, happy, social member of his class throughout the elementary grades. His fourth-grade teacher's comment seemed to apply to Wayne in all grades. She said, "He works very well in a group and will often be the backbone, the support of the group, because he willingly takes on the tasks necessary to bring the assignment to completion."

In response to a questionnaire in the second grade to the question, "Remember when you first started school? How did you feel?" Wayne said, "Oh, that was a long time back! I liked to play with blocks, then I went on to drawing, that's why I'm so good now." When Wayne was asked this question in the fifth grade he responded, "Terribly." In the sixth grade his answer to the same question was, "I felt afraid and wanted to go home."

In the second year during an Open School Week visit, his mother remarked, "It was worth sitting in school for *three* weeks to get Wayne started right." She expressed her gratitude for the aid the school had given in helping to overcome Wayne's problem in kindergarten. Not only was he doing well in school, he was getting along very well at home, too. When at the end of the sixth grade he was called up for an award at the closing assembly, his mother confided to the Project Assistant that her gratification was ample compensation for *the week* that she had spent in the kindergarten helping Wayne to get started, completely forgetting the long six weeks that she had spent in the kindergarten. Evidently, his mother's memory of early events was not quite as accurate at this time as was Wayne's.

Wayne moved out of the district at the end of the sixth grade and we can only assume that he continued to do as well.

The few children who subsequently developed persistent school phobias were not among those who showed separation problems in the kindergarten.

Jane L. was a quiet, reserved child of average intelligence, who came to school willingly in the kindergarten. She seemed to prefer seat activities and to play only with the little girl who sat next to her. As the term progressed she became more sociable, mixed with the children more freely, and related to the teacher increasingly. Although her speech was difficult to understand, she spoke a great deal about her sister, who was four years younger than she.

In the first grade, Jane cried and clung to her teacher each time the class went to the auditorium. Her mother traced this difficulty back to Jane's fear of the hearing test which was given in the kindergarten. For this test children had been taken to the auditorium a few at a time. Jane frequently cried at the beginning of the day and she became increasingly fearful. In Grade 2 she cried less often, but in Grade 3 she cried almost daily. She often complained of stomach pains and would cry at home before coming to school. She cried whenever her teacher was absent and children were sent to other classes, or when a substitute teacher was assigned to the class. Even after a class trip in which she participated one morning and about which she seemed enthusiastic, her mother had to urge her to return to school for the afternoon session.

The pattern was much the same in the beginning of the fourth grade and was further aggravated by "Sunday night illness" which she developed and for which her doctor had prescribed tranquilizers. Many of her absences were caused by spastic stomach difficulties which her doctor attributed to "nervousness." Jane was in the fourth grade when her sister entered kindergarten. Although her mother had at first brought the younger child to school each day, by November, Jane began to escort her sister to school. By midyear Jane seemed to be much better adjusted. There was no problem in getting her to come to school in the fifth or sixth grades, but she did cry easily. She was very sensitive and she cried hysterically when the children teased her about a mistake she had made during a dance rehearsal. She cried, too, when she was placed in a lower spelling group. By the middle of the sixth grade, however, her mother stated that Jane had a real desire to do her work, to come to school, and that she was having difficulty keeping her home when she was ill. It is interesting to note here that in a composition entitled "If I Could Fly," which was written in the fifth grade, Jane wrote, "I would find a school that is open every day because I like school."

On Parent Questionnaires in response to the question *Is there anything about school that worries your child?* Jane's mother answered:

Grade 1     "The monitors."
Grade 3     "Fear of substitute teachers."
Grade 6     "Tests and reading in front of the class."

Her responses to the question *Does your child usually like school?* were as follows:

Grade 1     "No."
Grade 3     "She dislikes going back to school on Monday. She likes her teacher and most of the children. She will not give a reason for her refusal to go."
Grade 6     "Yes."

Jane's sister was very much on her mind in the second grade when Jane responded during an interview in the following way:

*If you could have one wish what would it be?* "That my sister could go to school with me. Even if I have to take her, that's O.K."
*What do you wish you were?* "If Laura (sister) could be my age. I'd want to be her age. Her and me are just four years apart."
*When are you happy?* "When my sister plays with me."
*Remember when you first started school? How did you feel?* "I didn't like it so much. In kindergarten I did, but not in first grade."
*What do you remember about when you were in first grade?* "I was tired when I got home. Now I feel like running all over the house."

In Grade 6, when asked to complete statements on a questionnaire, Jane wrote, *The way I feel about school is* "happy." *What I did not like about elementary school*—"I liked the whole school."

Jane eagerly started junior high school, but after the first few days of school an incident in her social studies class upset her considerably. Her teacher had sent her to the blackboard to write an answer to a question, but Jane burst into tears. Crying hysterically, she was sent to see the guidance counselor, to whom she explained her sensitivity about her poor handwriting and about reciting in front of the class. After this experience Jane was reluctant to come to school, and so a conference was arranged between her mother and the guidance counselor. Jane's mother obtained clinical help for her and she was also seen regularly by the guidance counselor for the rest of the school year. She was made a monitor in the guidance office, which required her reporting to school early each day, a responsibility she took very seriously. With help and guidance she was able to complete the seventh grade successfully. Jane's attitude toward school was much improved during the next two years, and she freely sought advice from school personnel whenever she felt she needed it. She was graduated from junior high school and was admitted to a commercial course in high school.

Jane received remedial tutoring in English in high school and consistently passed all her subjects, sometimes with high grades. She received a progress award in accounting and an Honorable Mention Certificate for school service based upon her role as a member of the editorial board of her school newspaper. Her high school record shows no evidence of her previous difficulties and indicates that she was able to overcome her school phobia.

Jane responded to the questionnaire sent her when she was graduated from high school. In response to the question, *What do you think you'll be doing five years from now?* she answered with one word—"married." Jane fulfilled her aspirations and judging from her last letter, the word "happily" may be added.

As can be seen from the preceding tables, most children resolved their difficulties rapidly and successfully. The cases described are those where anxiety seemed to persist longest. In the total group listed in the tables are also included children who came to school with very severe problems, where separation anxiety was short-lived and formed only a small part of the total pattern of disturbance.

Gardner (1963) studied children with school phobias and concluded that girls outnumbered boys in presenting such problems. In reviewing the literature on anxiety and fears, Sarason et al. (1960) also found this to be the case. Our findings do not support these conclusions, for there were an almost equal number of boys and girls who showed separation anxiety.

It is very difficult to derive generalizations from these data. Perhaps the most important conclusion that can be drawn is that the appearance of great anxiety on being separated from a parent upon admission to school seems in no way predictive of subsequent maladjustment or adjustment, of failure or success. There is a strong indication from first-grade performance and from teacher observations that if the total group of those who had shown separation anxiety had remained with us for the entire seven-year elementary school period, a majority would have been among the well-adjusted, superior, achieving children in our study. Just why this is so, is difficult to determine.

For many years, the writer was a supervisor in several schools and made it a practice to visit kindergartens on the opening day of school. On the basis of many observations, it is hypothesized that aside from home background and personality factors, intellectually superior children are sensitive to many more aspects of the total environment than are average children and are therefore faced with many more unknowns. The average child can more easily become preoccupied with a specific toy or game or person.

This hypothesis is supported in a study of children's fears by Boston (1939). Boston found that 61% of the children of superior intelligence were reported to have fears compared with 36% of the children of average intelligence. Sarason et al. summarize Boston's study and state, "the fears of the superior children tend to result from a high sensitivity to subtle and covert danger cues from the environment, whereas the fears of less intelligent children tend to result only from the more blatant cues. Thus, the latter would have fewer fears because they are more or less 'immune' to the subtle and covert cues" (1960, p. 44).

Our own observations, over the years, of early separation anxiety led to the publication of a suggested orientation program (New York City Board of Education, 1957) which schools might use in helping their newly enrolled children at this milestone in their young lives. At the least, parents should be permitted to remain nearby as long as their children find it necessary, thus providing children with reassurance and with opportunities for participation in classroom activities as steps in facilitating adjustment.

# CHAPTER SEVEN

## Mobility

At the beginning of this project there was considerable skepticism concerning the advisability of including in a longitudinal study a school such as the Washington School with its high rate of mobility. It was generally felt that the chances were very slight that any of the children who began in the kindergarten would still be in the school at the end of the sixth grade. These fears were not altogether without foundation. The number of admissions and discharges during any one year in the Washington School varied from one-half to a number equal to and even above the total register of the school.

This excessive mobility is still one of the many problems plaguing urban school systems. The 1962 annual report of the reading program in the elementary schools of New York City stated:

In nearly a third of New York City's elementary schools, more than half the children will change schools one or more times during their elementary schools years. In Manhattan last year, more than half the schools (52% to be precise) suffered a "turnover" of half or more of the children enrolled in them. Consider the impact of this mobility on sequential development and continuity in teaching reading [New York City Board of Education, 1963, p. 5].

The same idea was expressed in an address by Max J. Rubin, former President of the New York City Board of Education, when he said:

During one school year in New York City, approximately 95,000 children will transfer from one school to another or more than one. There are dozens of classrooms in this city in which 35 children occupied seats on the opening day of school in September and by next June, 35 other children will be sitting in those seats, and between those two dates, other children, temporarily will have sat in those seats. Yet the teachers are called upon to provide a continuity in their education and these children, for the most part without roots, must be supplied not only with the tools of learning but with some degree of motivation for learning [1962].

Other cities have similar problems. In the school year 1965–1966 in the Los Angeles area, there were 117,419 pupil movements out of a total school enrollment of 306,792 children (Calvo, 1969).

Pupil turnover in the Jefferson School was comparatively small. Most of the group continued to live in the middle-income housing project adjacent to the school and moved only when families became larger and more space was needed. Some moved to apartments outside of the school district while others moved to larger houses in the suburbs. In the Washington School, the high rate of mobility gave the project staff considerable concern. There were some children who moved in and out of the neighborhood of the school as much as four times in a school year; others were gone for a few months or for a few years, while many moved away permanently after attending the school for only a brief period. The record cards of these children show such irregular and spasmodic schooling that it is difficult to understand how they received any degree of stability and how any learning took place. Some children moved from relative to relative, that is, from mother to aunt, to grandmother, and so on. Others moved just as frequently with their entire families.

The Washington School presented a unique situation in which to study mobility. The availability of data concerning all the children was only one factor. The other factor lay in the fact that the community maintained a reasonable degree of physical stability during the entire period of the study. Unlike similar neighborhoods in New York City, no provision had as yet been made for improved housing in this area. As a result, no demolition of houses took place and no new low-cost housing projects had been erected. As far as could be determined, the movement of families was in no way forced nor due to the need for compulsory relocation. It is therefore assumed that whenever a family moved out of the neighborhood, it was motivated by any combination or complex of factors that cause families on this socioeconomic level to change their residences with such frequency. Mobility thus presented itself as a problem *only* in the

Washington School and the following discussion is limited to an examination of the problem in this school.

In separating our basic children from those whom we identify as mobile, we find two distinct groups in the latter category. Of the 159 children on register in the Washington School at the end of the first grade, only 67 remained to finish the sixth grade. Another 13 children joined us in the second grade and were included in our basic population as explained in Chapter Two. The 92 children who left the school sometime after the first grade will be considered as one of the mobile groups. It was not within the scope of this study, nor was personnel available, to follow these children to their subsequent schools. It is therefore not known how frequently they moved after this first transfer and what degree of stability the family achieved. For purposes of this study, this group is considered one of the mobile groups and is identified as Mobile I, indicating that they were with us at least in Grade 1.

The other group that is considered mobile consists of those children who entered the school sometime after the beginning of the third grade and who were still with us in the sixth grade. More than half of these entered the Washington School with no records or with incomplete records, making it difficult to determine the number of schools previously attended. Less than half, however, did present complete records that show attendance in anywhere from two to ten schools in a six-year period. With this group, a question arises concerning the validity of our use of the word "mobility." There can be no question that a child who has attended ten schools in a six-year period shows high mobility. However, can the same be said of a child who has attended two or three schools during his elementary school years?

Since we have accepted as part of our basic population those children who joined the study at the beginning of the second grade and who had attended only one other school prior to this (in other words, a total of two schools), we would be unjustified in considering the children who joined us subsequently from *one* other school as being mobile. For purposes of this study therefore, mobility is attributed only to those children whose entrance into the Washington School represented at least their third school admission, and those children who came to the Washington School with incomplete records, where prior mobility is assumed, even though only two previous schools may have been recorded. This group is called Mobile VI, indicating that they were with us in Grade 6. Their mobility is shown in Table 7-1.

Turning to the first group (Mobile I), that is, those who started with

Table 7-1    Mobile VI Group—Number of Schools Attended Prior to Admission—Washington School

| Known Number of Schools Attended | N | Number of Pupils | | | | | | Otis Quick-Scoring Beta IQ | |
| | | Records Complete | | | Records Incomplete | | | | |
| | | Boys | Girls | Total | Boys | Girls | Total | Range | Score or Median |
|---|---|---|---|---|---|---|---|---|---|
| 10 | 1 | 1 | 0 | 1 | | | | | b |
| 9 | 2 | 1 | 1 | 2 | | | | | 94 |
| 8 | 1 | 1 | 0 | 1 | | | | | 86 |
| 7 | 2 | 0 | 1 | 1 | 0 | 1 | 1 | | 68 |
| 6 | 2 | 0 | 1 | 1 | 0 | 1 | 1 | | 79 |
| 5 | 6 | 1 | 4 | 5 | 0 | 1 | 1 | 55–95 | 82 |
| 4 | 7 | 1 | 2 | 3 | 1 | 3 | 4 | 72–107 | 82 |
| 3 | 23 | 9 | 9 | 18 | 4 | 1 | 5 | 68–128 | 83 |
| 2 | 33 | a | a | a | 18 | 15 | 33 | 58–118 | 91 |
| Total | 77 | 14 | 18 | 32 | 23 | 22 | 45 | | |

a Not considered mobile.
b Score missing.

us in the kindergarten or first grade but did not remain to complete the sixth grade, examination of our data raises some interesting questions. Were there any areas in which our basic population differed from this mobile population? As we greeted, observed, and interviewed our first-grade children and came to know them so well, were there any clues that we might have used to separate the two groups, to predict which of the children would remain basic and which destined to move away? Were there any inherent characteristics that distinguished one group from another? Examination of our first-grade data reveals some interesting differences.

In the second half of the first grade, children in all New York City schools were given the Pintner-Cunningham Primary Test as their first measure of intelligence. On this test, the group that was destined to become basic achieved a mean IQ of 98.59, whereas the potentially mobile group had a mean IQ of 93.63. This difference of approximately 5 points is statistically significant at the .05 level. The difference in mean IQs between the boys of the two groups was greater than that of the girls in the two groups.

A decade later, Frankel and Forlano (1967) reported similar conclusions when they studied differences in IQ scores between transient and nontransient New York City pupils who had been given the Otis Alpha

Test in the third grade and the Otis Beta Test in the sixth grade. They concluded: "The nontransient subgroup at the third grade score significantly higher on the Otis Alpha than their transient classmates. The same subgroup of nontransient pupils scored higher on the Otis Beta Test than another group of transient counterparts" (p. 357).

Somewhat earlier in the first grade, the New York Reading Readiness Test had been administered to help teachers assess the readiness of their children to begin a more formal program in reading. As has already been explained, this test has two parts. The first part asks teachers to evaluate each child's readiness for the reading process in terms of his maturity in the areas of physical, mental, social, and emotional development, and in relation to his language, and experiential background. In our basic group, 19 out of 80 children (23.7%) were considered unsatisfactory in one or more areas, while in the Mobile I group 55 of 86 (64%) were so designated. Table 7-2 presents this information.

Table 7-2    Teacher Ratings of Pupil Development
New York Reading Readiness Test—Part 1
Washington School, Grade 1

|  | N | All Satisfactory | | Unsatisfactory in 1 or More Areas | |
|---|---|---|---|---|---|
|  |  | N | Percentage | N | Percentage |
| Mobile I |  |  |  |  |  |
| Boys | 47 | 18 | 38.3 | 29 | 61.7 |
| Girls | 39 | 13 | 33.3 | 26 | 66.7 |
| Total | 86 | 31 | 36.0 | 55 | 64.0 |
| Basic |  |  |  |  |  |
| Boys | 32 | 24 | 75.0 | 8 | 25.0 |
| Girls | 48 | 37 | 77.1 | 11 | 22.9 |
| Total | 80 | 61 | 76.3 | 19 | 23.7 |

The figures in Table 7-3 indicate the incidence of unsatisfactory ratings in each area rather than numbers of children. Children who were unsatisfactory in one or more areas are recorded separately in each of the categories.

The second part of the test requires children to carry out on their test papers instructions given orally by teachers. Ratings are given in percentiles. On this test the mean score for the mobile children was 43.73 and for the basic children 56.06. Here again, the difference is statistically

**Table 7-3   Incidence of Unsatisfactory Ratings in Areas of Development**
**New York Reading Readiness Test—Part 1—Washington School, Grade 1**

| | Total N [a] | Physical | | Mental | | Social | | Emotional | | Language | | Experience | |
|---|---|---|---|---|---|---|---|---|---|---|---|---|---|
| | | N | Percentage | N | Percentage | N | Percentage | N | Percentage | N | Percentage | N | Percentage |
| Mobile I | | | | | | | | | | | | | |
| Boys | 47 | 9 | 19.1 | 10 | 21.3 | 14 | 29.8 | 15 | 31.9 | 6 | 12.8 | 15 | 31.9 |
| Girls | 39 | 4 | 10.3 | 11 | 28.2 | 8 | 20.5 | 9 | 23.1 | 4 | 10.3 | 8 | 20.5 |
| Total | 86 | 13 | 15.1 | 21 | 24.4 | 22 | 25.6 | 24 | 27.9 | 10 | 11.6 | 23 | 26.7 |
| Basic | | | | | | | | | | | | | |
| Boys | 32 | 2 | 6.3 | 2 | 6.3 | 1 | 3.1 | 1 | 3.1 | 3 | 9.4 | 5 | 15.6 |
| Girls | 48 | 4 | 8.3 | 4 | 8.3 | 1 | 2.1 | 2 | 4.2 | 5 | 10.4 | 6 | 12.5 |
| Total | 80 | 6 | 7.5 | 6 | 7.5 | 2 | 2.5 | 3 | 3.8 | 8 | 10.0 | 11 | 13.8 |

[a] Includes both Satisfactory and Unsatisfactory.

significant at the .01 level, with the boys of the two groups showing a greater mean difference than the girls.

It would seem, from these figures, that the potentially mobile children as a group demonstrated greater immaturity in most areas of development than did the basic children, and that in the objective portion of the test, they indicated less readiness for the formal reading program.

With New York City's large non-English-speaking population, one is tempted to jump to the conclusion that it is this group that accounts for the poorer performance of the mobile population. However, this is not the case here at all. The ethnic composition of the total first-grade group shows comparatively few Hispanic and other non-English-speaking children. Furthermore, the *only* area where the mobile and basic children were similar was that of language background, as can be seen in Table 7-3.

At the end of the first grade all children were given the New York Inventory of Mathematical Concepts for Grade 1. On this test the Mobile I group achieved a mean score of 41.98 and the basic group of 51.80. This difference is also significant.

It should be emphasized that these differences, although analyzed 10 years later, were present at the very start of the journey through school. Examination of other measurements and observations made in the first grade reveal similar results.

For reasons that do not lend themselves to analysis, these two groups also differed in the number of adjustment problems they presented in the first grade. Of the 47 Mobile I boys, 18 were reported by their teachers as adjustment problems. This represents 38.3% of the total number of these boys. Of the 32 basic boys, only 4 (12.5%) indicated problems of adjustment. The two groups of girls also showed differences in the number of adjustment problems reported, but here again the difference between the two was smaller than between the Mobile I and basic boys. Of the 39 girls in the Mobile I group, 3 (7.7%) were listed as adjustment problems. Of the 48 basic girls, only 2 (4.2%) were so reported in the first grade. These data are shown in Table 7-4.

Adjustment differences between the mobile and basic groups seem to lie not in the types of problems presented, but rather in their number.

The question arises as to whether there were factors completely outside of the school that might also have distinguished the basic children from those who were to become mobile. For one thing, there were disrupted homes from which children of both groups came to school. A good deal of this information was available at registration time while additional and supplementary information was obtained during the course of the first year. Could disrupted homes (as previously defined)

**Table 7-4    Adjustment Problems—Washington School, Grade 1**

|  | | Problems | |
|---|---|---|---|
|  | N | N | Percentage |
| Mobile I | | | |
| Boys | 47 | 18 | 38.3 |
| Girls | 39 | 3 | 7.7 |
| Total | 86 | 21 | 24.4 |
| Basic | | | |
| Boys | 32 | 4 | 12.5 |
| Girls | 48 | 2 | 4.2 |
| Total | 80 | 6 | 7.5 |

be related to subsequent mobility? Table 7-5 indicates that in the Mobile I group 16 of the 47 boys (34.0%) and 12 of the 39 girls (30.8%) or a total of 32.6% came from disrupted homes. In the basic group, five of the 32 boys (15.6%) and 19 of the 48 girls (39.6%) came from homes that may be considered disrupted. This represents 30.0% of the total. It would seem, however, that the incidence of disrupted homes does not differentiate between the two groups and, at least quantitatively, this can be ruled out as a significant factor related to mobility.

**Table 7-5    Incidence of "Disrupted" Homes on Entrance into Study Washington School**

|  | | Disrupted Homes | |
|---|---|---|---|
|  | N | N | Percentage |
| Mobile I | | | |
| Boys | 47 | 16 | 34.0 |
| Girls | 39 | 12 | 30.8 |
| Total | 86 | 28 | 32.6 |
| Basic | | | |
| Boys | 32 | 5 | 15.6 |
| Girls | 48 | 19 | 39.6 |
| Total | 80 | 24 | 30.0 |

Other specific data available concerning children's homes were those pertaining to the occupations of the heads of the household. Much of Warner's Scale for rating socioeconomic class could not be applied to our urban population. An attempt was made to use only a portion of this scale, but this proved impractical for our purposes and was not

sufficiently discriminating in classifying different levels of similar occupations. A revised occupational scale for rating socioeconomic class by Hamburger (1958) proved to be of greater value with our families. This scale
is a seven-level scale in which the same occupational groups are repeated
on most of the levels. The level assigned, however, is dependent on the
educational training, prestige, and/or income required for that occupation. For example, Level 1 contains those professional occupations that
require high responsibility and usually postgraduate training, often at
the doctorate level. Professional occupations on Level 3 include those
professions in which a bachelor's degree or less is sufficient. The same
categories with examples are given for semiprofessional occupations,
business occupations, clerical, sales, manual work, protective and service
workers, and farmers. The application of this scale showed that the children who were to become basic came from families whose breadwinners
scored at a somewhat higher socioeconomic level than those families that
became mobile, with a difference that is significant at the .05 level.

Delving further into possible differences between the two groups,
we might examine enrollment in the kindergarten. Table 7-6 shows that
34 (39.5%) of the 86 Mobile I children attended kindergarten, whereas
52 (60.5%) did not. In the basic group the proportions are generally re-
versed with 51 (63.8%) of the 80 attending kindergarten and 29 (36.3%)
children not attending.

**Table 7-6    Kindergarten Experience**
**Mobile I and Basic Population—Washington School**

|          | N  | Attended Kindergarten | | Did Not Attend | |
|----------|----|-----|------------|----|------------|
|          |    | N   | Percentage | N  | Percentage |
| Mobile I |    |     |            |    |            |
| Boys     | 47 | 20  | 42.6       | 27 | 57.4       |
| Girls    | 39 | 14  | 35.9       | 25 | 64.1       |
| Total    | 86 | 34  | 39.5       | 52 | 60.5       |
| Basic    |    |     |            |    |            |
| Boys     | 32 | 21  | 65.6       | 11 | 34.4       |
| Girls    | 48 | 30  | 62.5       | 18 | 37.5       |
| Total    | 80 | 51  | 63.75      | 29 | 36.25      |

As has been mentioned previously, attendance in the kindergarten
was not always within the control of parents. In some schools there were
not enough classrooms to provide for all the children. However, since
children were accepted into kindergartens in the order in which they

had registered, it would seem that those children who were to become the basic population and remain in the school had gained admittance to kindergarten by registering earlier than those who were mobile. It may be concluded that parental eagerness for children to attend school was greater among the stable population.

Let us turn now to the other mobile group (Mobile VI). This group includes all children who entered our basic children's classes at any time after the beginning of the third grade and who were still with us in the sixth grade, having attended three or more schools prior to their admission, or having been admitted to the Washington School with incomplete records. Using the scores obtained on the Otis Quick-Scoring Beta Test which was administered in the sixth grade, we find that the mean IQ of the Mobile VI population was 85.3, whereas the mean IQ of the basic population was 97.34. This difference of approximately 12 points is statistically significant at the .05 level. On this group test in the sixth grade, the greater difference was found between the girls rather than between the two groups of boys, as had been the case in the first grade. Comparing the two groups on the Metropolitan Achievement Intermediate Reading Test which was also administered that year, we find that the Mobile VI group had a mean grade score of 5.2 and the basic group had a mean grade score of 6.0. Although this difference is statistically significant, there may be a reasonable doubt as to whether it is an educationally significant difference. One would expect reading to be the best index of achievement in school and one of the first areas to be affected by irregular schooling. The results are therefore somewhat surprising and difficult to account for.

The only other achievement test administered on a citywide basis in the sixth grade was the Metropolitan Achievement Intermediate Mathematics Test. On this test the mean grade score for the Mobile VI group was 5.8 and for the basic group was 6.6. This difference is also statistically significant, but what is surprising here is that the mobile group scored as high as they did.

Comparisons of parental occupations of the two groups in this grade showed no significant differences.

Where possible, the same factors that had been used for the Grade 1 population were used in examining differences among the Grade 6 populations. Data on kindergarten enrollment were inconclusive because of the large number of incomplete records. Whereas (Table 7-7) only eight out of the 77 (10.4%) Mobile VI children had attended kindergarten and 20 (26%) had not, 51 of the 80 (63.8%) basic children had attended kindergarten. The remaining 49 (63.6%) Mobile VI children entered the Washington School with such incomplete records that the determination of kindergarten attendance was not possible.

Table 7-7    Kindergarten Experience
             Mobile VI and Basic Population—Washington School

|  | | Attended Kindergarten | | Did Not Attend | | No Record | |
|---|---|---|---|---|---|---|---|
|  | N | N | Percentage | N | Percentage | N | Percentage |
| Mobile VI | | | | | | | |
| Boys | 37 | 5 | 13.5 | 8 | 21.6 | 24 | 64.9 |
| Girls | 40 | 3 | 7.5 | 12 | 30.0 | 25 | 62.5 |
| Total | 77 | 8 | 10.4 | 20 | 26.0 | 49 | 63.6 |
| Basic | | | | | | | |
| Boys | 32 | 21 | 65.6 | 11 | 34.4 | — | — |
| Girls | 48 | 30 | 62.5 | 18 | 37.5 | — | — |
| Total | 80 | 51 | 63.8 | 29 | 36.25 | — | — |

When teachers in the sixth grade were asked to list children with adjustment problems, 9 of the 37 Mobile VI boys (24.3%) and 5 of the 40 Mobile VI girls (12.5%) were reported as problems; in the basic group, 9 of 32 boys (28.1%) and 7 of 48 girls (14.8%) were so reported. Neither in the number reported nor in the types of adjustment problems presented did there seem to be more than slight variations between the groups. The data in Table 7-8, which are often inconsistent and frequently contradictory, do not suggest any clear-cut conclusions.

Table 7-8    Adjustment Problems—Grade 6—Mobile VI
             and Basic Population—Washington School

|  | Total | Problems | |
|---|---|---|---|
|  | N | N | Percentage |
| Mobile VI | | | |
| Boys | 37 | 9 | 24.3 |
| Girls | 40 | 5 | 12.5 |
| Total | 77 | 14 | 18.2 |
| Basic | | | |
| Boys | 32 | 9 | 28.1 |
| Girls | 48 | 7 | 14.6 |
| Total | 80 | 16 | 20.0 |

Summarizing our findings concerning the Mobile I population, we find that of the total first-grade group, the children who were to stay with us and who were to form our basic population showed from the start a higher mean IQ, greater maturity in those traits considered necessary for the beginning of reading, higher mean scores on a reading readiness test and on a mathematical concepts test than did the children who were to leave us. Furthermore, children in the basic group presented fewer problems of adjustment and came from families on a somewhat higher socioeconomic level. Almost twice as many of the basic children had attended kindergarten as compared with the mobile group. The only area on the New York Reading Readiness Test where there seemed to be no significant difference between the basic and the mobile groups was that of language background, which includes not only knowledge of English but a general assessment of vocabulary knowledge and fluency. There was also no difference in the number of disrupted homes.

At the sixth-grade level, the basic group was also superior in mean IQ to the Mobile VI group, but it was only slightly although significantly superior to it in both reading and mathematics. Parental occupations showed no important differences, and missing data prevented any conclusions concerning kindergarten attendance. There was also little difference between the basic and Mobile VI groups in the number and types of adjustment problems presented.

The considerable number of differences already existing in Grade 1 between the two groups would lead us to expect as many or even greater differences between the Mobile VI and the basic group. Yet this is not so. Furthermore, comparatively good performances in both mathematics and reading of the Mobile VI group is entirely inconsistent with our general experience in New York City schools, where children who have transferred from city to city and from school to school are usually considerably below more stable children in their general achievement.

Studies of children in nonurban communities support our Mobile VI findings but not our general experience. Snipes (1966) tested reading vocabulary and reading comprehension among sixth-grade pupils in a county in central Georgia and concluded that, "The number of moves pupils make does not appear to have a detrimental effect on achievement in reading" (p. 245). Stiles (1968) measured achievement among transient and nontransient children of military personnel and found no significant difference in achievement in reading and arithmetic.

A study reported by Greene and Daughty (1961) on school mobility involved 434 members of the junior class of Savannah High School in Savannah, Georgia. They compared "recency of mobility," "distance of mobility," and "school mobility," with students' marks in school subjects on the California Test of Mental Maturity and on the California Achievement Tests, as well as several other tests. Greene and Daughty report general superiority in all areas in grades, attendance, and punctuality of the mobile students as compared with those who were more stable in their residential patterns.

In order to reconcile our findings both with expectations and with experience, further evaluations were undertaken. The neighborhood of the Washington School has already been briefly described. It might be helpful, however, to take another look at the general community as it was, in an effort to determine its place not only in comparison with other communities and neighborhoods in New York City but also in terms of the socioeconomic picture it presented to the black community of New York and the degree of its desirability or undesirability as a place of residence. As has been mentioned before, the Washington School was located in the upper part of Manhattan on the fringe of Harlem. Demographic maps did not classify this area among those on the lowest socioeconomic level; nevertheless, approximately one-third to one-half of its children qualified for free lunch. The neighborhood has wide streets, many open areas, and is quite close to a park. It is far less congested than central Harlem and gives the impression that its residents live on a somewhat higher socioeconomic level. The buildings were old but in better repair than many in the Harlem area, and many still showed evidence of architectural ornateness. The neighborhood might better be classified as a section of the city which, in the early decades of this century, had become a center of lower-class population in its striving for upward mobility. This area also included in those decades the homes of economically and professionally successful blacks who were able to leave behind them the traditional centers of Negro residence.

Like so many other neighborhoods in urban centers, this one had deteriorated considerably. Fine residences and well-kept apartment houses in the school district were rare. Many large apartments had been broken up into smaller ones, and with more families and an increased population, the neighborhood had suffered considerable attrition.

In an effort to determine the status symbol of this neighborhood to the Harlem black, conferences were held with principals of Harlem schools, with black teachers, and with others who could help us with valid interpretations. There was general consensus that, in spite of the changes that had taken place, it still represented an area to which blacks aspired to move in an effort to better their social environment and to provide a better community in which to bring up their children.

On the basis of these conclusions, it is hypothesized that our Mobile VI population represented social and economic upward mobility and, as our occupational comparison has shown, these children had come to the Washington School district with parents who had improved their status and who were the equals of their longer resident neighbors. If we assume that such families bring with them better attitudes toward learning and school, and thus give greater motivation to their children, then we can perhaps explain the superior achievement shown by our Mobile VI children.

This assumption is supported by Gordon (1970) in reviewing research on socially disadvantaged children. He states, "Evidence from the Coleman Report and a number of other sources supports the conclusion that home conditions, general conditions of life, are more important predictors of school achievement than any of the variables that were studied" (p. 10). Luszki and Schmuck (1965) note that pupils who perceive their parents as holding supportive attitudes toward school, utilize their abilities more fully, have more positive attitudes toward school, and have higher self-esteem than pupils who perceive less parental support.

How, then, can we explain the lower IQs and the lower level of performance of our Mobile I children? For this group, it is hypothesized that their families found themselves in a neighborhood where they were unable to sustain themselves either economically or socially, and from which they moved sooner or later. Both of these hypotheses are borne out, to some extent, by an examination of former and subsequent residences. On the basis of available data, it seems that the majority of Mobile VI children had moved from more depressed areas into this comparatively better community. No conclusions can, of course, be drawn for those children who had come from another city.

To the extent that data were available, the hypothesis concerning Mobile I children also held up. A good many of these children moved out of the area into more congested, lower socioeconomic sections of the city. It is again assumed here (and not without considerable hesitation) that intelligence and the many other factors that account for achievement in school are found to a lesser degree where downward mobility is indicated.

In studies done several years later, Morris et al. (1967), arriving at similar conclusions, state:

An upwardly mobile family having itself learned or acquired the necessary functional value system, will transmit it to its children. The children would then have fewer problems in adapting to a new social and educational milieu. . . .

Families which are downward mobile may rear children who are less well equipped to deal with the pressures of new and demanding situations [p. 79].

It would seem that mobility itself had less effect on the growth and achievement of our children than did the causes of mobility. These findings are true for the Washington School, which may not be a completely typical inner-city school. There is no intent here to generalize, nor do we know whether a similar study in another school would have produced the same conclusions.

# CHAPTER EIGHT

## Selected Findings

It was inevitable that a 20-year period of observations and collection of data would produce a wealth of material far too great to fully describe. It is hoped that the topics discussed in previous chapters touch upon major aspects of child growth and development. Like the exposed parts of an iceberg, however, they rest upon a much greater mass of rich qualitative material made up of the astute observations of the staff, the sometimes profound comments of children, and the spontaneous reactions of the adults, both parents and educators, who were involved in the educational process.

Included in this chapter are items that seem pertinent to the total investigation. Topics have been arbitrarily selected as being interesting or significant.

### REACTION TO CLASS SIZE

During the first three grades, children in the Jefferson School were grouped among four classes with registers ranging from 24 to 31 children per class. At the end of the third grade, the school lost one teaching position and, as a result, the same number of children were divided among three classes on each grade beyond the third. Class registers in the fourth, fifth, and sixth grades thus varied from 37 to 39.

Frequent discussions between the Project Assistant and teachers included many spontaneous reactions to the larger registers. Their impressions probably can best be presented by quoting comments made toward the end of the school year by three fourth-grade teachers:

The large register gives me feelings of inadequacy. I'm failing my class and there's nothing I can do about it. Some days I go home and think about my day in school and realize that I haven't spoken to some children at all.

I was trained to believe and do know that individual help is very much worthwhile, but I get too little opportunity to give it. I'm resentful because I'm always rationalizing that I can't do this in a class of 38. Children are entitled to some special help, but this can only be done before 8:30 and after 3:00 P.M., and I don't like to interfere with a child's normal day, though I frequently do.

I always seem to have an allegiance to another group when I'm working with one group. The poorest readers need individual help, their security is threatened, especially since they came from a special class of 24 where they were able to receive more individual attention.

Equally valid are the Project Assistant's objective observations of the effects of larger registers upon children and teachers:

Many of the children who had never been singled out as adjustment problems before are listed as such in the fourth grade. These are children who are insecure, and who need constant assurance. They floundered for the first few months.

Some of the brightest in the grade haven't been challenged sufficiently. Teachers say that some of those interested in science, electronics, and so on, are lost in the group.

Some children who aren't aggressive, aren't demanding, are just lost.

Teachers have lost some of the closeness with many of the children.

Activities seem to be more structured than before. There is much more group instruction most of the time.

Much of the creative work seems to have suffered. Teachers have given children less opportunity for creative expression because large group activities consume so much more time.

### TESTS AND TESTING

There is great need for a reorientation program for teachers and supervisors concerning the purposes and the uses of standardized tests. For one thing, there seems to be considerable misunderstanding about what tests do and do not measure; for another, there is confusion about the meaning of a norm.

It would be completely irrelevant to discuss these topics here, but when a grade norm is interpreted as a standard of attainment for all pupils, the effects upon children may be profound. On the basis of staff observations, one may also question strongly the practice by teachers and supervisors of publicly announcing in class the test achievement scores obtained by each child.

When children are told that they are deficient until they meet the grade norm, the anxiety which is triggered sometimes becomes a paralyzing force and frequently shows its effects well into the high school years (Kirkland, 1971). It is as if we were to line up children in the order of their scores, set the norm at the midpoint, and then proceed to punish all the children who are below this point—although we used them to establish that midpoint or norm. Chauncey and Dobbin describe this misconception as follows: "too many teachers have built the word 'norm' into their vocabulary with a wrong connotation; with this erroneous view, 'below the norm' means the same as 'sub-normal' and has all sorts of emotional consequences that are both inaccurate and unfortunate" (1963, p. 47). To some of our children, the announcement of a grade score considerably below the norm was thus a source of discouragement and deep humiliation, which was not always internalized.

Such procedures had other effects. The concentration of Jefferson School children in a nearby housing project produced not only closer friendships but also greater competitiveness among the children. Relationships among different families and adults were also inevitably closer. Thus any child's score on a test was known to many more children and adults than was the case in the Washington School, and the announcement of test scores was greeted with far greater apprehension.

A by-product of such pressure to achieve on tests was its effect on teachers. In another study (New York City Board of Education, 1962) conducted concurrently with this one, the project staff had opportunities to visit more than 100 schools in New York City. In all schools, especially in the fifth and sixth grades, there was a direct relationship between test achievement pressures and a noticeable decrease in opportunities provided children for creative expression. Supervisory pressure for more drill in reading and mathematics was inevitably accompanied by decreasing attention to art, music, dramatics, and poetry.

Frequent emphasis should be given to Chauncey and Dobbin's statement that "Even the very best test is good only when used for a specific purpose with the kind of students for whom it was intended. . . . No test can be universally good, equally appropriate and useful for many purposes and all students" (1963, p. 54). They indicate further that the best tests are only samples of behavior and that no final decision about any student can be made solely on the basis of one test score.

## TEACHERS AND THE STUDY

By the time the children had completed the sixth grade, the project staff had worked closely with 24 teachers in the Jefferson School and 42 in the Washington School. The good relationships that were consistently developed do not lend themselves to description, but the enthusiasm and interest of the teachers whose children were being studied warrant comment and commendation.

Running as a thread through countless discussions was teachers' appreciation of the opportunity to discuss their children with well-informed, receptive, professional colleagues who were not part of the school staff and who were not judgmental in their approach. Teachers also reacted positively to the fact that substitutes were employed to "cover" their classes so that the biweekly hourly meetings with Project Assistants could be carried on without tension or pressure to hurry back to class.

The following truly representative comments, which were neither encouraged nor solicited, give some indication of the impact of the study upon teachers of the first six grades:

I have taken so many psychology courses and background courses, have had the material, but never before have I been able to put it to such use. Now everything has come to life.

This catharsis—just talking out, discussing certain cases is so helpful.

In the discussion we are given an opportunity to air ourselves—talking about these children helps us see things more clearly. To discuss children with someone who is not critical and who knows the children and is not supervisory in attitude, is so helpful.

I always had *classes* before, now I have individual children.

I never knew you could get to know so much about each child in your class. Talking about each child, rating him on each of the scales, certainly gives you a real picture.

I've really had to stop and think and look at individuals. Usually it's only a certain few I've gotten to know.

It's important to know as much as possible about children in order to help them. School records don't seem to be enough. This study has made me aware, and has provided so much additional information, that I feel I could write a book about each child.

I realize now how much more there is to a child than what I used to see.

One must hasten to add that interest and enthusiasm among junior high school teachers and guidance counselors was equally high even though staff-teacher conferences were held far less regularly and less frequently. Here, teachers sought out the one remaining Project Assistant, and in their free periods they eagerly endeavored to learn more about the children whom they were teaching.


## PARENTS AND THE STUDY

It is very difficult to differentiate between parental response to the study and response to the personalities of the Project Assistants. Relationships with some parents were first started when they registered their children for kindergarten or first grade. Others were greeted informally during the year as they brought their children to school. At some time during the kindergarten year and again during the first grade, principals informed parents at Parent Association meetings that their children were involved in a study and they explained briefly and very generally its scope and purpose.

The next contact with parents occurred toward the end of the first grade when a questionnaire was sent home. With very few reminders and with very little prodding there was a 91% return in the Jefferson School and a 75% response in the Washington School. These numbers are well beyond the expected returns for this type of material and indicate the interest and degree of cooperation that was being given. Questionnaires were again sent to parents in the third and sixth grades where responses in the Jefferson School climbed to 100% and in the Washington School to 90%.

Perhaps of greater importance than the quantity of returns was the eagerness of many parents to confer with Project Assistants. To the question, "Do you want to meet with the Project Assistant?" asked in the first-grade questionnaire, an affirmative answer was given by 29% of Jefferson School parents and 35% of Washington School parents. For a variety of reasons not all of the parents of the Washington School who requested appointments availed themselves of the opportunity. As the years went by an increasing number of parents sought the occasion to consult with Project Assistants. These included not only parents of children with problems but also of those who were doing well both at home and in school.

Appointments were then made and there began several years of unanticipated conferences with parents which involved discussion, perhaps guidance, sometimes referrals to community agencies, and always a receptive setting in which parents could allay anxiety by discussing their children.

These conferences were not only fruitful for the study, but they were of great value to parents. They pointed up strongly the need for personnel who were not part of the regular school staff, but to whom parents could turn for advice or for comfort. As indicated earlier, budgetary limitations after the first seven years left the study with only the one Project Assistant who had served the Jefferson School. After 10 years, she was still being sought out by parents whose children were then in the tenth and eleventh grades in high schools.

## THE PHYSICAL DEVIATES

During the entire course of the study, a record was kept of the obvious physical deviates, that is, the tallest in each class, the shortest, the obese, and all children who were handicapped or who deviated in some observable way from the physical norm of the classes. Such children also included the stutterers and the orthopedically handicapped.

Here, too, the presence of physical deviations did not seem to be related to achievement or adjustment, and whatever effects they may have had on personality were not overtly observable as influencing functioning in the normal school situation. This is contrary to the findings of MacFarlane (1938), who studied children over a 10-year period and observed that oversized or undersized children had greater problems of adjustment than did children of normal size and development.

## HANDEDNESS

There was neither trained personnel nor equipment available to measure laterality among our children. All notations of handedness were the results of staff observations in classroom situations and of hand preferences in executing simple tasks. In the primary grades, each child was observed as he bounced and threw a ball, used scissors, and opened a door, and note was made of our left-handed and right-handed children.

Throughout the course of the study, no child was observed to have changed his hand preference, nor was there any evidence of parental pressure on left-handed children. There was, however, no way of knowing what changes had been forced during the preschool period, and attempts to question parents about this phase of their children's growth proved fruitless. Nevertheless, staff observations may have had considerable validity. Harris (1947) indicates that throwing a ball is influenced relatively little by training and it may be that the tasks mentioned did actually measure laterality more or less effectively.

Conceding the crudity of the measures, and our inability to detect incomplete lateral dominance, and noting the fact that only 15% of our children were left-handed, it appears that left-handedness among our children seemed to be unrelated to academic success or failure, to adjustment or maladjustment. In fact, a larger percentage of left-handed children were found among the achievers and the well adjusted than among the children who were having difficulties.

### THE DAY THE SCHOOL BURNED DOWN

Among the many unanticipated incidents and events that occurred was the total destruction of the Washington School by fire. On the morning of October 28, 1958, a five-alarm fire broke out and by the time the children had arrived for classes, much of the school, although still burning, was already gutted. The five-story brick school building had been erected in 1890 and had been partially modernized in 1900. It had been slated for replacement and was fairly high on the city's priority list. When the fire broke out, the study had already been under way for more than five years.

Within minutes after the fire had started, word of the conflagration was passed on by telephone throughout the night from custodian to principal, from teacher to teacher, and so, along with the teachers, the Project Assistants were at the school before 7:30 on the morning of the fire to assist in whatever way they could. The sheer drama of the situation, however, made them realize that the role of impartial observer would be too fruitful to abandon completely.

By 10:00 A.M., principals and teachers were meeting in the office of the field superintendent, where superb organizational skills and the self-lessness and eager cooperation of school personnel resulted in detailed plans to reopen classes the very next day. More than a mile away, a recently vacated school had been scheduled for demolition. Within an hour, plans had been made to reopen this school building and to bus all the children to and from this school daily.

The impact of a burning school building upon our children and the response of the school staff to the emergency can best be described by the following log recorded by the Project Assistants:

TUESDAY, OCTOBER 28

2:50 A.M.    Five-alarm fire destroys the Washington School.

8:30 A.M.    Children and teachers arrive at school. Children react to the loss of their school in many ways. Some cry. Others look stunned and bewildered. A few seem glad to have a "holiday."

One kindergarten child faints when he sees the ruined building.

A first-grade child looks up at the still smoldering school. He turns to his mother. "Isn't it lucky that I took my note-book home with me last night?"

A third-grader: "Why did it have to burn down? I loved that school."

A second-grader: "It was the nicest school in the whole world!"

A third-grade boy to his teacher: "Our books!" he cries. "All our books are in there!" His teacher puts her arm around his shoulder. "We'll get new books," she promises, "nice, new books. Don't worry about it."

A fourth-grader to his teacher as they look up at the re-mains of their room (the ceiling had caved in): "Look!" he cries, "Our flag! It's still waving. It's like a miracle."

Another fourth-grader to her teacher: "If you can get back into the building will you *please* get my arithmetic book."

A worried-looking group of fifth-graders are saying: "What will happen to us if all the records burned up? How will we get into junior high without records?" "And how about all those reports we wrote—all our story reports?" "And our envelopes with all our written work . . . I wonder did they get burned up too?"

Sixth-graders: "I've been here since kindergarten—now I won't be able to graduate from the Washington School." Several adults from the neighborhood stand around. They recall the days when they had attended the school.

From the teachers:

Teacher after teacher remarks, "Isn't it lucky there were no children in the building? Imagine if it had happened during school time!"

"All my wonderful library books! I've been collecting them for years. They're all gone."

"We finally finished our book inventories. Now we have no inventories and no books either."

"Billy's puppets! He brought all his puppets to school yesterday."

"My kids just finished the most wonderful chart about the U.N. They worked so hard on it, too. Now it's gone."

A sense of deep loss seems to hit one teacher after another. A typical remark: "I know it was an old building but I loved it."

Many teachers speak of the additional materials they have brought to school (3-speed record players, recordings, books, magazines, pictures, games, souvenirs from trips, toys their own children had outgrown, etc.).

10:00 A.M.    Teachers are called to a conference in the office of the field superintendent. Parents from the local school, which houses the office, are on hand with a large urn of hot coffee. Teachers are told that emergency housing will be provided at a recently vacated school. New classrooms are assigned by the principal.

Teacher reaction:

"At least we'll all be under one roof."

"I'm so glad that our classes won't be broken up."

"It will take me a half hour longer to get to and from school. I'll have to set the alarm for 6 o'clock now, but I don't mind because we're together."

"Will it be safe for the children?"

"I've been in this school all my life (from a teacher eligible for retirement). I can't imagine teaching any place else, but I guess I'll get used to it."

1:00 P.M.    Teachers report to new locations and become acquainted with the building and their home rooms.
After seeing their new classrooms teachers remark:

"It took a fire to do it but I finally have a closed room (no rolling doors). All my walls stay in one place!"
"This room is much lighter and airier than my old one."
"A piano! I have a piano in my room."
"You know what I found? I have a *sink* in my room. It will be so much easier to have painting and clay work."
"You should see the wall space I have. Now I have room for the children to work on a mural."
"I have much more blackboard space here."

1:30 P.M.    Conference is called by the principal to plan the opening of school on the following day. Entire reorganization has been completed and is presented to the teachers who comment:

"It will be a terrific job to bus over 1600 children from one school to another."
"What about the children who used to go home to lunch? Can we feed them too?"
"It will take hours to load all the children on busses. We should start earlier."
"I know it will be a hardship but there's no other way out. We'll have to give up our lunch hour and eat with the children in our own rooms. We can't send them out into a neighborhood that's strange to them."

WEDNESDAY, OCTOBER 29

8:00 A.M.    Several teachers meet the children at the site of the burned school and help to load the children into the busses which shuttle between buildings until all the children have been transported.
A teacher rides in each bus and answers the children's questions. A child is crying. The teacher tries to reassure her and the other children. "When you get to your new school, your same teacher and your own classmates will be waiting for you. You will all be together again. A bus will take you back, after school, to the same place you left from this morning. Isn't it fun to ride a bus to school every

morning and back again every afternoon?" The children agree enthusiastically.

8:10 A.M.    Children from a school adjacent to the temporary quarters greet the children and their teachers with placards of welcome and emergency packages of school supplies. The children are escorted into the yard where they are met by their teachers.

The first day in their new quarters teachers tell anecdotes such as the following:

"At 9:30 a teacher from the adjacent school came looking for me. She had her whole class with her. She told me that she had been in the very room I now have, for many, many years, and that she liked my room much better than her new one in the new school. Each of her children carried something as a 'housewarming gift.' They brought paper, crayons, scotch tape, plants, pencils and erasers. Each child was carrying something."

"Did you see the welcoming committee in front of the school this morning? There was a whole class with a teacher. Some children had big placards saying, 'Welcome, Neighbors' and 'Welcome to Your New Home.' The rest of the children were holding plants and packages of paper."

"Yesterday we were visited by a teacher and class from a nearby school. They brought us all sorts of wonderful things—construction paper, pencils, paper, and a big, big Halloween witch for a wall decoration. My children wrote them the most beautiful thank-you letters."

Specific incidents of a similar nature are reported by teachers.

Offers of help come from other schools in the neighborhood, from a representative from Harlem Hospital, and from the Assemblyman's office.

The following letter is sent by a fourth-grade class in the nearby school:

October 30, 1958

Dear Friends,

We know since your school burned down and you have to travel by bus you cannot have a Halloween Party so we would like to invite you over to our party from 1:15

to 2:30 on Friday, October 31st so there will be time for you to get back to your classroom and get your books and catch your bus. We will be very glad to have you.

Your friend,
Susan L.

Anxious parents accompany their children to the new location. The principal invites them to walk through the building and to reassure themselves of its condition. There are many murmurs of approval and expressions of satisfaction. Parents are also helpful to the teachers whose reactions may be summed up as follows:

"The parents have been wonderful. They come around and serve hot coffee and cookies. How we need it . . . not so much the coffee but just the feeling they're with us and trying to make life a little easier."

10:00 A.M.     A child asks, "Mrs. ———— when we write our heading do we still write Washington School?" "Of course you do, you are still in the Washington School even though we are in another building. We're all together here—all the children, the teachers, the principal, and even the custodial staff and the lunchroom workers." The children spontaneously applaud.

These incidents and reactions, which will surprise many, are not limited to our basic children but represent the spontaneous outpourings of concern from children in all grades, from parents, from the community. This was a so-called inner-city, ghetto school with an 85% black pupil population. The statements quoted are not the result of careful selection and editing but are typical of the drama that unfolded. We do not know whether children in the middle-class Jefferson School would have reacted similarly.

How can we reconcile the behavior described here with Silberman's (1970) description of schools? These children did not respond as victims of a "grim, joyless" place, "oppressive and petty, . . . intellectually sterile and esthetically barren, . . . an appalling lack of civility . . . on the part of teachers and principals, [with] contempt they unconsciously display for children as children" (p. 10).

One must conclude that children do not see their schools in the same perspective as do adults. Adults have frequently overlooked the fact that the organization and structure of the school give many disadvantaged children a sense of stability and security to a degree which they do not enjoy in their homes. For the most part, expectations are clear and limits have been delineated. For those who are achievement motivated, the school is an avenue to the fulfillment of aspirations.

There is no attempt here to generalize. This is a description of a specific population in a specific situation. Fifteen years have elapsed since the school burned down. The social strife and pressures of the last decade have had a profound impact upon children and upon their attitudes toward school. Whether the scenes described would be reenacted today in a similar way is beyond our ability to conjecture.


## SIMPLE QUESTIONS AND PROFOUND ANSWERS

The reader will recall that during the first seven years of the study, the children's reactions to a variety of topics were obtained from oral and written interviews and from compositions written on specific subjects.

The quality of the many responses obtained on these occasions eludes description. One can only emphasize that many of the answers reflected a spontaneity, an unintentional whimsy and humor, and sometimes a profundity characteristic only of children. Some of these responses are presented here in conclusion of this report of a study which was for the project staff also an adventure in learning.


### From Interviews

*Remember when you first started school? How did you feel?* (Grade 2)
"I feyt I wished I wasn't."

"I felt scared. Because it was all these strange people at school. The only person I wasn't afraid of was the teacher."

*What do you remember about when you were in Kindergarten?* (Grade 2)

"I don't remember nothin'. I was too smart to go to Kindergarten."

"We got cookies for free, now we have to buy them."

"I think I was playing in the sandbox. Boy, they sure kept you busy."

*What do you wish you were?* (Grade 2)

"First I want to go in the army. When I come out I want to be a policeman on a horse—a mountee. I asked one, 'How do you get to be a mountee?' He say, 'You got to have a clean record.' And I got a clean record so far."

*What don't you like in school?* (Grade 2)

"I don't like to write or read. I don't hardly like to do anything but go up and downstairs with messages."

"I think it's thirds and fourths."

## From Written Questionnaires

*What do you remember about when you were in the first grade?* (Grade 3)

"When I used to wash the boards and do these numbers and examples 1 and 1 and 2 and 2 but I really didn't know them—I counted on my fingers."

*What do the children like best about you?* (Grade 3)

"I don't know. Maybe because they elected me vice-president. They really didn't, 'cause they were bad, so teacher picked me."

*What do you like best about yourself?* (Grade 3)

"I'm honest . . . teacher says. When I have to fight I have to fight."

## From Handwriting Samples (Written Compositions)

*If I Had Ten Dollars* (Grade 3)

"I would support my family good and buy my baby sister that isn't even born yet, some clothes and for me a parakeet."

*If I Could Fly* (Grade 4)

"I think to fly is better for the birds than for people."

*If I Were A Teacher* (Grade 6)

"If I were a teacher I would quit the job. If you have a bad class it's nerve racking."

"About 5 or 6 years at teaching I would resign and that would be enough and I would get another job."

"My class rules would be:
1. Let them have a talking period twice a day.

2. Don't be cruel with them they are only children.
3. Don't only teach them but have fun with them.
4. Let everybody be one big happy family. don't let anyone be put out. remember everyone is a life itself and everyone wants to be wanted at school and at home. Thank you."

# CHAPTER NINE

Summary and Conclusions

Neither at its inception nor at any time during the ensuing 20 years was it the purpose of this study to give suggestions to schools. We had hoped only to present the results of measurements and intensive observations of children, thus giving schools an opportunity to examine the data, to determine its significance for them, and to make whatever adaptations they wished in terms of their own organizations, goals, and pupil populations.

Readers of the previous chapters will realize that we may have overstepped our original intent. In some areas, the implications were loud and clear; in others, our own deep involvement provided qualitative insights which we would have been remiss to have omitted. This chapter, therefore, summarizes quantitative data previously described and adds conclusions derived from observations of the immeasurables and the intangibles, from conversations, from the dynamics of classroom situations, and from years of interaction with children, parents, and teachers.

### Measurements of Intelligence

So-called deterioration of IQ, where subsequent intelligence tests show decreasing IQ scores, occurred only among children whose original IQ scores were above 110. This was characteristic of both schools and seemed

141

unrelated to socioeconomic environment. In no case did the observed learning pattern or level of performance change to parallel recorded changes in IQ.

Changes in recorded IQs were probably a result of the different intelligence tests that were administered. Correlations between those given in the elementary school years varied from .41 to .89 (see Appendix, Tables 1—4).

Teachers' reliance on IQ scores and their concepts of their importance have been greatly exaggerated. At no time during the elementary and junior high school years did an IQ score determine promotion or retention, or class placement or rejection in the ordinary class. These administrative decisions were based solely on class performance, usually interpreted in terms of reading achievement. The only exception occurred in admission to the Special Progress classes where Board of Education directives required a minimum IQ of 125. However, all children who were otherwise eligible succeeded in obtaining the required minimum IQ.

Furthermore, contrary to the conclusions of Rosenthal and Jacobson (1968), teachers' knowledge of IQ had no effect on teacher expectancy or pupil performance. Several studies have been cited which support our findings, as does a recent study by Jose and Cody (1971).

### Reading Achievement

In the Jefferson School, a larger percentage of boys than of girls read below the norm until the fourth grade, when boys as a group surpassed girls. In the Washington School, a larger percentage of boys than girls scored consistently below the norm in all grades.

The most significant measure was the score obtained on the third-grade reading achievement test. There is a high correlation between this score and all subsequent reading, mathematics, and intelligence test scores and with general performance on the junior and senior high school level. There were no "late bloomers" and for most of our children in both schools, third-grade reading achievement might have been used for purposes of prediction even beyond the high school years.

Depressing as this conclusion may be, it is corroborated by two other studies. Bloom (1964) notes:

The first period of elementary school (grades 1 to 3) is probably the most crucial period available to the public schools for the development of general learning patterns. We are inclined to believe that this is the most important growing period for academic achievement and that all subsequent learning in the school is affected and in large part determined by what the child has learned by the age of 9 or by the end of grade 3 [p. 110].

Husen's (1969) longitudinal study in Sweden also points up the significance of third-grade performance. He found that teachers' ratings and intelligence test scores in the third grade were good predictors of subsequent educational careers.

## Tests and School Marks

There is a general misunderstanding among teachers and administrators concerning the meaning of grade norms. They are frequently interpreted as minimum standards for attainment, and they are used as such. In approaching the junior high school years, the pressure for achieving at or above the grade norm from both parents and teachers had considerable impact on the total teaching program and upon children, making the program far more rigid and limited in depth and scope, and filling the children with deep anxiety.

It is this misunderstanding which led Dyer, of the Educational Testing Service, to label grade equivalency scores as "psychological and statistical monstrosities." He finds no fault with the content of tests, which are at best, "never more than a sample of a student's performance and is therefore inevitably subject to sampling error" (1971, p. I–10), but he does criticize the interpretation of grade equivalency scores.

More destructive of teacher morale and pupils' self-image is the practice of the New York City Board of Education of publishing in the newspapers each year the grade equivalency scores obtained in the annual achievement testing program by each grade in every school. It is unrealistic to expect parents to understand that statistically, half the children will always fall below the norm, no matter how well they actually read. This has resulted, in recent years, in odious comparisons between schools, and miltant attacks upon teachers and supervisors by parents of children in schools with low reading scores.

## Retention

Of the 33 children who were held back in a grade at some time in their elementary school years, only two gained more than a year in reading ability as measured by standardized achievement tests. Almost all the others gained less during the year in which they repeated the grade than they did during the years of promotion, and several were judged to have developed serious problems of adjustment after having been retained.

## Acceleration

Almost all of the children who were accelerated did so by admission to Special Progress classes in junior high schools, where they completed the curriculum of the seventh, eighth, and ninth grades in two years and performed very well. Superior achievement by accelerated children was characteristic of their progress through the high school and college years.

## Giftedness and Talents

Special gifts and talents were discovered, for the most part, either by teachers who possessed these gifts themselves or who provided programs of such depth and variety that children had opportunities to demonstrate special talents. Where programs of instruction were narrow and limited, few children were identified as being gifted. Nevertheless, consistent superior performance or demonstration of talent was recognized early. Children who were listed three or more times as being talented or creative in art, music, or dramatics had been so identified before the end of the second grade.

## Adjustment

Most of the children reported as having adjustment problems in any one of the early grades remained problems and were subsequently reported by two or more teachers. Furthermore, all but three of those reported in the sixth grade had displayed their difficulties before the end of the third grade and continued to have problems in the junior high schools and well beyond. This persistence of behavioral patterns is also noted in a longitudinal study by Kagan and Moss, who state: "It would appear that, for some children, the first four years of contact with the school and peer environments (i.e., during ages 6 to 10) crystallize behavioral tendencies that are maintained through young adulthood" (1962, p. 272).

The most sensitive predictor of maladjustment seems to have been the New York Reading Readiness test, which was administered early in the first grade, before most children had even been identified as being seriously maladjusted. There was a 17 to 19.6 difference in percentile rating in favor of those who were to adjust well as compared to those who were to have adjustment and behavior problems during the following nine years.

## Traumatic Experiences

No single traumatic experience seemed to alter the observable pattern of learning or behavior of our children. Those who had had severe traumatic experiences were able to cope with their problems and maintain their accustomed levels of performance in the school environment.

## Separation Anxiety and School Phobia

Children who had difficulty leaving their mothers upon admission to kindergarten and who showed great anxiety were representative of the entire basic population. Neither intelligence nor subsequent achievement test scores distinguished them from the other children. These groups in both schools included the subsequent successes and failures, the mature and well adjusted, as well as those who were destined to be consistently identified as adjustment problems. The total original group of children in this category were, in fact, slightly superior in ability and performance as compared to our study population.

## Mobility

This was a problem only in the Washington School, where it was found that of the total first-grade group, the children who were to stay with us and who were eventually to form our basic population showed from the start a statistically significant higher mean IQ, greater maturity in those traits considered necessary for beginning reading, higher mean scores on a reading readiness test and on a mathematics concepts test than did the children who were to leave us. Furthermore, children in the basic group presented fewer problems of adjustment. Almost twice as many of the basic children had attended kindergarten as compared with the mobile group.

Another group that was examined consisted of children who transferred into the Washington School after the first grade after having attended three or more other schools. The basic group was significantly, but only slightly superior in mean IQ and achievement test scores. There was little difference between the groups in the number and types of adjustment problems presented. It is hypothesized that the surprisingly good academic performance of this second mobile group is related to social and economic upward mobility of their parents.

### Black Children and Black Teachers

One aspect of the civil rights revolution has been the increasing demand for more black teachers and the assumption that black children would then identify more easily with their teachers, and therefore make better adjustments and better progress in school. Edmund W. Gordon, Professor of Education at Teachers College, Columbia University, effectively expresses this view. He writes:

> If cultural and ethnic identification are important components of the learning experience, to ignore or demean them is poor education.
> If curriculum and delivery systems do not take these factors into account, inefficient learning may be the result. One would hope that black education by black educators is not the only solution, yet we are being pressed to no longer ignore it as a possible solution [1971, p. 75].

There were several black teachers in the Washington School, which most of our black children attended, but none in the Jefferson School. A careful examination of the records of our black children during their entire elementary school experience in the Washington School fails to disclose any differences in adjustment, achievement, or general academic progress during the years when they were in the classrooms of black teachers as compared to white teachers. We fully realize that measures of ethnic identification require highly sensitive instruments, and that achievement tests, school marks, and adjustment scales are very crude measures for this purpose. Nevertheless, the black and white children who had both black and white teachers did not seem to have growth experiences identifiably and noticeably different because of the ethnic differences of their teachers.

Upon graduation from high school, 14 black children in the study, distributed among six different high schools, returned questionnaires. We are reasonably certain that at least nine of them had had a black teacher at some time in their high school careers. In answer to the question, "What characteristics would you like to see in a teacher?" several named specific teachers and described them, whereas others gave descriptions so vivid, that the teacher was easily identifiable. Two of the nine answers did not lend themselves to identification.

We thus had seven children who described with affection seven different teachers, some from their elementary or junior high school days, who had had profound effects upon them. In none of the descriptions was there any reference to color or race, and in no case did these seem to be factors in children's choices. From the kindergarten through the twelfth grade in high school, there is no evidence that either black or white teachers were necessarily better for either black or white children. It was the particular characteristics of the teachers rather than their color that made the difference.

## Children's Drawings and Self-Images

It will be recalled that each year from 1953 to 1960, children had been asked to draw pictures of themselves or of anybody. During this entire time not one black or Puerto Rican or white child added color to the face in his drawing. In 1972, the writer asked 25 white teachers and five black teachers to have their classes draw pictures of themselves, giving children the identical instructions used in our study.

Of 170 black children, 96 blackened their faces. Of 164 Puerto Rican children, 24 darkened their faces, but two whitened the faces of their drawings with chalk. The 50 Oriental children also were aware of ethnicity; almost all drew Oriental features and 21 darkened their faces. Of the white children, 9 of 195 whitened the faces of their sketches, but two white children darkened their faces heavily. There was no difference in responses of children in classes with black or white teachers.

The reader must draw his own conclusions from these data. We are inclined to feel that in the 1950s children thought of themselves and each other as children and were hardly aware of differences in color. The motivations which caused black children to blacken their faces, Puerto Rican children to darken or whiten their faces, and white children to seek out chalk or, in two cases, to blacken their faces, indicate that children have been deeply affected by current racial issues. There are many implications here which need exploration and which should provide considerable food for thought.

## Classrooms—Structured and Open

The Open Classroom, described and lauded by Silberman (1970) and Weber (1971), did not exist as such by name when our children were in the elementary grades. Nevertheless, the structure of the 66 classrooms in which our children found themselves during their elementary school years varied to a great extent with each teacher's teaching style. The project staff spent many hours each year in the classrooms of all these teachers and it was thus possible to rank each one on a somewhat crude scale from highly structured, rigid, and inflexible to flexible, creative, loosely structured, and open. The word "open" does not here have the connotation given it by Weber, for at the time of this study, some aspects of the current open classroom were not available to either teachers or pupils.

Nevertheless, the classrooms we describe as open gave children many opportunities for exploration and growth, and provided highly creative learning experiences. Examining our children's records for growth in achievement and adjustment, we again find that although these classes were satisfying and stimulating for most children, not all children necessarily made better progress while in such classes. What is most significant is that children who came from unstructured homes seemed to find safety and comfort in more structured classrooms, whereas those whose homes were better organized were better able to handle the flexibility and effectively utilize the many opportunities for growth and learning in the less highly structured, open classrooms.

### The High School Experience—Student Evaluation

One of the many questions we asked our youngsters upon their graduation from high school was, "Are you satisfied with your achievement in high school? Please explain." Among those who answered *Yes* and those who answered *No* were some who had done well and some who had done poorly. It is interesting to note that many more were dissatisfied than satisfied with their performance in high school. Of the children who had originally come from the Washington School, only 16 returned the questionnaire, and of these, two were satisfied and 14 dissatisfied with their high school achievement. Many of the dissatisfied thought that they could have done better had they been more serious or applied themselves more diligently. Others regretted that they had not chosen a different course.

Of the 48 respondents who had started in the Jefferson School, 18 were satisfied and 30 dissatisfied with their achievement in high school. The dissatisfied group mentioned most often failure to work up to potential. A number of children who were not outstanding were, nevertheless, satisfied with their achievement. Their responses are typified by the student who wrote, "I may not have done too well, but I did my very best and that meant working up to my capacity."

The questionnaire also included, "Are your parents satisfied with your achievement in high school?" In both groups all parents of the satisfied youngsters agreed with their children's evaluations, but three-fourths of the parents of the dissatisfied indicated that they accepted their children's achievement as satisfactory.

Qualitatively, some of the dissatisfied children's responses revealed deep regret, frustration, and remorse, and a few were quite poignant. For example:

I feel that I could have achieved much more if I had worked harder and did less fooling around.

If I really had known what I wanted to be, I could have achieved more.

I could have done better if I had a little more quiet in the house.

I wanted to receive an academic diploma and go to college, but because of the separation of my parents, my studies fell off and I had to change my course. I'm undecided what I'll do for a living. Maybe I can learn a trade in the army.

## Parental Aspirations

Several studies have shown that parental aspirations of lower-class and middle-class parents are very similar. Cloward and Jones (1963) report lower-class parents indicating education as important to their children, and Weiner and Murray (1963) also report that low and middle-class socioeconomic parents both have high levels of aspiration for their children's education. We asked our parents, when their children were in the sixth grade and again when they were in the ninth grade, whether they expected their children to go to college. Jefferson School parents could be described as lower middle-class, Washington School parents as lower-class, but the responses of all parents in both schools were definitely positive. To the question, "What would you like him/her to do for a living?" the most common response in both schools was, "Anything that will make him (her) happy." Similarities in aspirations of parents of children in both schools were overwhelmingly greater than differences. Race and color were completely irrelevant factors.

# EPILOGUE

Our children are now grown men and women. Among them are teachers and students of law, dentistry, and medicine; technicians and nurses, secretaries and clerks, salesmen and budding junior executives, housewives and mothers, mechanics and skilled laborers. Among them, also, are the failures in life—the drifters and the adult delinquents. It is futile to speculate which aspects of their lives were shaped by school experiences. Certainly the organizational changes that occurred during their schooling seemed to have no measurable effect. We can only wonder which of the successes of children can be attributed to the school, and which of the failures can be laid at its feet. How do we really know when the school has succeeded and for what it can be held accountable?

We hope that this study points up the need for continuing longitudinal studies to search out further cause-and-effect relationships, and that such studies will be recognized as important research tools in formulating sound educational policies. It is paradoxical that a nation that has carried on extensive research in child growth and development frequently ignores it in developing educational practices.

# REFERENCES

Abidin, R., W. M. Golladay, and A. Howerton, 1971. Elementary school retention: an unjustifiable, discriminatory, and noxious educational policy. *Journal of School Psychology,* **9,** 4, 410–417.

Anderson, J. E., et al., 1959. *A Survey of Children's Adjustment over Time.* Minneapolis: NIH Project M690.

Anderson, S. B., 1961. *ETS Developments,* **10,** 1, 1–4.

———, 1969. The ETO-OEO longitudinal study of disadvantaged children. *Untangling the Tangled Web of Education.* Princeton: Educational Testing Service.

Anfinson, R. D., 1941. School progress and pupil adjustment. *Elementary School Journal,* **41,** 507–514.

Baldwin, B. T., 1921. The physical growth of children from birth to maturity. *University of Iowa Studies in Child Welfare,* **1,** 1.

Bayley, N., 1933. Mental growth during the first three years: A developmental study of sixty-one children by repeated tests. *Genetic Psychology Monographs,* **14,** 1–92.

———, 1940. Factors influencing the growth of intelligence in young children. *Intelligence: Its Nature and Nurture,* Part 2. 39th Yearbook of the National Society for the Study of Education. Bloomington, Ill.: Public School Publishing Co.

———, 1949. Consistency and variability in the growth of intelligence from birth to eighteen years. *Journal of Genetic Psychology,* **75,** 165–196.

———, 1955. On the growth of intelligence. *American Psychologist,* **10,** 805–818.

———, 1964. Consistency of maternal and child behaviors in the Berkeley Growth Study. *Vita Humana,* **7,** 73–95.

———, 1968. Behavioral correlates of mental growth: Birth to thirty-six years. *American Psychologist,* **23,** 1, 1–17.

———— and H. E. Jones, 1937. Environmental correlates of mental and motor development: A cumulative study from infancy to six years. *Child Development*, **8**, 329–341.

———— and E. S. Schaefer, 1964. Correlations of maternal and child behaviors with the development of mental abilities: Data from the Berkeley Growth Study. *Monograph of the Society for Research in Child Development*, **29**.

Bloom, B. S., 1964. *Stability and Change in Human Characteristics*. New York: John Wiley and Sons.

Boston, M. V., 1939. Some factors related to the expression of fear in a group of average and superior children. *Smith College Studies in Social Work*, **10**, 106–107.

Breckenridge, M. E. and E. Lee Vincent, 1960. *Child Development*. Philadelphia: W. B. Saunders Co.

Bronson, W. C., 1969. Stable patterns of behavior: The significance of enduring orientations for personality development. In J. P. Hill (Ed.), *Minnesota Symposia on Child Psychology*, Vol. 2. Minneapolis: University of Minnesota Press.

Burks, B. S., D. W. Jensen, and L. M. Terman, 1930. *Genetic Studies of Genius: III. The Promise of Youth: Follow-up Studies of a Thousand Gifted Children*. Stanford: Stanford University Press.

Calvo, R. C., 1969. Helping the mobile child in school. *Phi Delta Kappan*, **50**, 8, 487.

Caswell, H. L., 1933. *Non-promotion in Elementary Schools*. Nashville, Tenn.: George Peabody College for Teachers.

Chauncey, H. and J. E. Dobbin, 1963. *Testing: Its Place in Education Today*. New York: Harper and Row.

Clairborn, W. L., 1969. Expectancy effects in the classroom: A failure to replicate. *Journal of Educational Psychology*, **60**, 5, 377–383.

Cloward, R. and J. Jones, 1963. Social class: Educational attitudes and participation. In A. H. Passow (Ed.), *Education in Depressed Areas*. New York: Teachers College Press, pp. 190–216.

Coffield, W. H. and P. Blommers, 1956. Effects of non-promotion on educational achievement in the elementary school. *Journal of Educational Psychology*, **47**, 235–250.

Coleman, J. S., 1966. *Equality of Educational Opportunity*. Washington, D.C.: U.S. Dept. of Health, Education, and Welfare.

Dearborn, W. F., J. W. Rothney, and F. K. Shuttleworth, 1938. Data on the growth of public school children. *Monograph of the Society for Research in Child Development*, **3**, 1–136.

Dechant, E. V., 1970. *Improving the Teaching of Reading*. Englewood Cliffs, N.J.: Prentice-Hall.

Dobbs, V. and D. Neville, 1967. The effect of non-promotion on the achievement of groups matched from retained first graders and promoted second graders. *Journal of Educational Research*, **60**, 472–475.

Dyer, H. S., 1971. The role of evaluation. *Proceedings of the Conferences on Educational Accountability*. Princeton: Educational Testing Service.

Ebert, E. and K. Simmons, 1943. The Brush Foundation study of child growth and development. *Monograph of the Society for Research in Child Development,* 8, 2.

Farley, E. S., A. J. Frey, and G. Garland, 1933. Factors related to the grade progress of pupils. *Elementary School Journal,* 34, 186–193.

Fleming, E. S. and R. G. Anttonen, 1971. Teacher expectancy or My Fair Lady. *American Educational Research Journal,* 8, 2, 241–252.

Frankel, E. and G. Forlano, 1967. Mobility as a factor in the performance of urban disadvantaged pupils on tests of mental ability. *Journal of Educational Research,* 60, 8, 355–358.

Freeman, F. N. and C. D. Flory, 1937. Growth in intellectual ability as measured by repeated tests. *Monograph of the Society for Research in Child Development,* 2, 2.

Gallagher, J., 1964. *Teaching the Gifted Child.* Boston: Allyn and Bacon.

Gardner, G. E., 1963. The child with school phobia. *Post-graduate Medicine,* 34, 3, 294–299.

Gerberich, J. R. and M. J. Blaha, 1961. Using test results to make decisions about pupil placement, grouping, and promotion. *The National Elementary Principal,* 41, 2, 18–21.

Gesell, A. L., 1926. The influence of puberty praecox upon mental growth. *Genetic Psychology Monographs,* 1, 511–539.

———, 1928. *Infancy and Human Growth.* New York: The Macmillan Co.

———, 1940. The stability of mental-growth careers (Chap. VIII). *Intelligence: Its Nature and Nurture,* Part 2. 39th Yearbook of the National Society for the Study of Education. Bloomington, Ill.: Public School Publishing Co.

———, C. S. Amatruda, B. M. Castner, and H. Thompson, 1939. *Biographies of Child Development: The Mental Growth Careers of Eighty-four Infants and Children; a Ten-Year Study.* New York: Hoeber Publishing Co.

——— and L. B. Ames, 1937. Early evidence of individuality in the human infant. *Scientific Monthly,* 45, 217–225.

——— and ———, 1947. The infant's reaction to his mirror image. *Pedagogical Seminary and Journal of Genetic Psychology,* 70, 141–154.

——— and F. L. Ilg, 1943. *Infant and Child in the Culture of Today.* New York and London: Harper and Bros.

——— and ———, 1946. *The Child from Five to Ten.* New York and London: Harper and Bros.

———, ———, and L. B. Ames, 1956. *Youth; the Years from Ten to Sixteen.* New York and London: Harper and Bros.

——— and H. Thompson, 1941. Twins T and C from infancy to adolescence; A bio-genetic study of individual differences by method of co-twin control. *Genetic Psychology Monographs,* 24, 3–121.

Ginsburg, H., 1972. *The Myth of the Deprived Child.* Englewood Cliffs, N.J.: Prentice-Hall.

Glasser, W., 1969. *Schools without Failure.* New York: Harper and Row.

———, 1971. *The Effect of School Failure on the Life of a Child.* Washington, D.C.: National Education Association.

Glavin, J. P., 1972. Persistence of behavior disorders in children. *Exceptional Children*, **38**, 5, 367–376.

Gold, M. J., 1965. *Education of the Intellectually Gifted*. Columbus, Ohio: Charles E. Merrill Books.

Goodlad, J. I., 1952. Research and theory regarding promotion and non-promotion. *Elementary School Journal*, **53**, 3, 150–155.

Gordon, E. W., 1970. Education for socially disadvantaged children. *Review of Educational Research*, **40**, 1, 1–12.

————, 1971. Are our schools too conservative to teach minorities effectively? *The New York Times*, January 11, 1971.

Greene, J. E. and S. L. Daughty, 1961. Factors associated with school mobility. *Journal of Educational Sociology*, **35**, 1, 36–40.

Hamburger, M., 1958. A revised occupational scale for rating socioeconomic class. *Realism and Consistency in Early Adolescent Aspirations and Expectations*. Unpublished doctoral dissertation, Columbia University.

Harris, A. J., 1947. *How to Increase Reading Ability*. New York: Longmans, Green and Co.

———— and R. J. Lovinger, 1968. Longitudinal measures of the intelligence of disadvantaged Negro adolescents. *School Review*, **76**, 60–66.

Hauck, B. and M. Freehill, 1972. *The Gifted—Case Studies*. Dubuque, Iowa: William C. Brown Co.

Havighurst, R. J., et al., 1962. *Growing up in River City*. New York: John Wiley and Sons.

Heilman, A. W., 1967. *Principles and Practices of Teaching Reading*. Columbus, Ohio: Charles E. Merrill Books.

Hilton, T. L. and C. Patrick, 1970. Cross-sectional versus longitudinal data: An empirical comparison of mean differences in academic growth. *Journal of Educational Measurement*, **7**, 1, 15–24.

Hunt, J. McV., 1961. *Intelligence and Experience*. New York: Ronald Press.

Hunter, E. C., 1957. Changes in teachers' attitudes towards children's behavior over the last thirty years. *Mental Hygiene*, **41**, 3–11.

Hurlock, E., 1972. *Child Development*, 5th ed. New York: McGraw-Hill Book Co.

Husen, T., 1969. *Talent, Opportunity and Career*. Stockholm: Almqvist and Wiksell.

Jersild, A. T., 1968. *Child Psychology*. Englewood Cliffs, N.J.: Prentice-Hall.

Johnson, R. C. and G. R. Medinnus, 1969. *Child Psychology: Behavior and Development*. New York: John Wiley and Sons.

Jones, H. E. and N. Bayley, 1941. The Berkeley Growth Study. *Child Development*, **12**, 167–173.

Jose, J. and J. J. Cody, 1971. Teacher-pupil interaction as it relates to attempted changes in teacher expectancy of academic ability and achievement. *American Educational Research Journal*, **8**, 1, 39–49.

Kagan, J. and H. A. Moss, 1962. *Birth to Maturity*. New York: John Wiley and Sons.

Kaplan, L., 1965. *Foundations of Human Behavior*. New York: Harper and Row.

Kirkland, M. C., 1971. The effects of tests on students and schools. *Review of Educational Research,* **41,** 4, 303–350.

Klineberg, O., et al., 1957. Race and intelligence. *World Mental Health,* **9,** 87–89.

Kowitz, G. T. and C. M. Armstrong, 1961. The effect of promotion policy on academic achievement. *The Elementary School Journal,* **61,** 8, 435–443.

Lavin, D. E., 1965. *The Prediction of Academic Performance.* New York: Russell Sage Foundation.

Leacock, E. B., 1969. *Teaching and Learning in City Schools: A Comparative Study.* New York: Basic Books.

Luszki, M. B., and R. Schmuck, 1965. Pupil perceptions of parental attitude toward school. *Mental Hygiene,* **49,** 296–307.

MacFarlane, J. W., 1938. Some findings from a ten-year guidance research program. *Progressive Education,* **15,** 529–535.

————, 1964. Perspectives on personality and change from the guidance study. *Vita Humana,* **7,** 115–126.

Mallinson, G. G. and J. Weston, 1954. To promote or not to promote. *Journal of Education,* **136,** 5, 155–158.

McElvee, E. W., 1936. A comparison of personality traits of 300 accelerated, normal, and retarded children. *Journal of Educational Research,* **16,** 31–34.

Mitchell, J. C., 1942. A study of teachers' and mental hygienists' ratings of certain behavior problems in children. *Journal of Educational Research,* **36,** 292–307.

Morris, J. L., M. Pestaner, and A. Nelson, 1967. Mobility and achievement. *Journal of Experimental Education,* **35,** 4, 74–80.

Murphy, L. B., 1964. Factors in continuity and change in the development of adaptational style in children. *Vita Humana,* **7,** 96–114.

National Education Association, 1950. *Advantages and Disadvantages of Non-failure Policy.* Washington, D.C.: Research Division of the National Education Association.

New York City Board of Education, 1941. *Final Report of the Speyer School (Public School 500).*

————, 1947. New York Reading Readiness Test, *Manual of Directions.*

————, *Division of Elementary Schools Circular,* 1955–1956, B.P. 21; 1956–1957, B.P. 16; 1957–1958, B.P. 20; 1958–1959, B.P. 17; 1959–1960, B.P. 30, et al. Mimeographed.

————, 1957. *Report of Orientation Programs in Kindergarten and First Grade.*

————, 1962. *Skillful Teaching Practices in the Elementary Schools,* Curriculum Bulletin No. 12, 1961–1962 Series.

————, 1963. The reading program in the elementary schools, *Annual Report, 1961–1962.* Mimeographed.

Oden, M. H., 1968. The fulfillment of promise: Forty-year follow-up of the Terman gifted group. *Genetic Psychology Monographs,* **77,** 3–93.

Osborne, R. T., 1960. Racial differences in mental growth and school achievement: A longitudinal study. *Psychological Reports,* **7,** 233–239.

Otto, H. J. and D. M. Estes, 1960. Accelerated and retarded progress. In C. W. Harris (Ed.), *Encyclopedia of Educational Research*, 3rd ed. New York: The Macmillan Co.

Pegnato, C. and J. Birch, 1959. Locating gifted children in junior high school. *Exceptional Children, 25,* 300–304.

Polos, N. C., 1965. *The Dynamics of Team Teaching.* Dubuque, Iowa: William C. Brown Co.

Redl, F. and W. W. Wattenberg, 1951. *Mental Hygiene in Teaching.* New York: Harcourt, Brace and Co.

Rohwer, W. D., 1971. Learning, race, and school success. *Review of Educational Research, 41,* 3, 191–210.

Rosenthal, R. and L. Jacobson, 1968. *Pygmalion in the Classroom.* New York: Holt, Rinehart and Winston.

Rubin, M. J., 1962. The Public and Its Schools. *Address,* Fifth Avenue Association Luncheon, November 15, 1962.

Rubin, R. and B. Balow, 1971. Learning and behavior disorders: A longitudinal study. *Exceptional Children, 38,* 4, 293–299.

Sandin, A. A., 1944. *Social and Emotional Adjustment of Regularly Promoted and Non-promoted Pupils.* New York: Bureau of Publications, Teachers College, Columbia University.

Sarason, S. B., 1970. *The Culture of the School and the Problem of Change.* Boston: Allyn and Bacon.

———, K. S. Davidson, F. F. Lightfall, R. R. Waite, and B. K. Ruebush, 1960. *Anxiety in Elementary School Children.* New York: John Wiley and Sons.

Saunders, C. M., 1941. *Promotion or Failure for the Elementary School Pupil?* New York: Bureau of Publications, Teachers College, Columbia University.

Scribner, H. B., 1971. *The New York Times,* January 30, 1971, p. 30.

Shirley, M. M., 1933. The first two years; A study of twenty-five babies, Vol. 2. *Institute of Child Welfare Monograph Series,* Nos. 6–8, Minneapolis: University of Minnesota.

———, 1938. Development of immature babies during their first two years. *Child Development, 9,* 347–360.

———, 1939. A behavior syndrome characterizing prematurely born children. *Child Development, 10,* 115–128.

———, 1942. Children's adjustments to a strange situation. *Journal of Abnormal and Social Psychology, 37,* 201–217.

——— and L. Poyntz, 1941. Development and cultural patterning in children's protests. *Child Development, 12,* 347–350.

Shuey, A. M., 1958. *Testing of Negro Intelligence.* Lynchburg, Va.: J. P. Bell Co.

Silberman, C. E., 1970. *Crisis in the Classroom.* New York: Random House.

Snipes, W. T., 1966. Effect of moving on reading achievement. *The Reading Teacher, 20,* 3, 242–246.

Sontag, L. W., C. T. Baker, and V. L. Nelson, 1958. Mental growth and personality development: A longitudinal study. *Monograph of the Society for Research in Child Development,* 23, 68, 1–143.

Steadman, E. R., 1959. Fifteen who were not promoted. *The Elementary School Journal,* 59, 5, 271–276.

Stein, L. and M. Susser, 1970. Mutability of intelligence and epidemiology of mild mental retardation. *Review of Educational Research,* 40, 1, 29–64.

Stennett, R. G., 1966. Emotional handicap in the elementary years: Phase or disease? *American Journal of Orthopsychiatry,* 36, 444–449.

Stiles, G. E., 1968. Families on the move. *The Educational Forum,* 32, 4, 467–474.

Stouffer, G. A. W., Jr., 1952. Behavior problems of children as viewed by teachers and mental hygienists: A study of present attitudes as compared with those reported by E. K. Wickman. *Mental Hygiene,* 36, 271–285.

Strom, R. D., 1969. *Psychology for the Classroom.* Englewood Cliffs, N.J.: Prentice-Hall.

Tanner, L. N. and H. C. Lindgren, 1971. *Classroom Teaching and Learning.* New York: Holt, Rinehart and Winston.

Terman, L. M., et al., 1925. *Genetic Studies of Genius: I. Mental and Physical Traits of a Thousand Gifted Children.* Stanford: Stanford University Press.

—— and M. H. Oden, 1947. *Genetic Studies of Genius: IV. The Gifted Child Grows Up: Twenty-five Years' Follow-up of a Superior Group.* Stanford: Stanford University Press.

—— and ——, 1959. *Genetic Studies of Genius: V. The Gifted Group at Midlife: Thirty-five Years' Follow-up of the Superior Child.* Stanford: Stanford University Press.

Thomas, A., S. Chess, and H. G. Birch, 1968. *Temperament and Behavior Disorders in Children.* New York: New York University Press.

Tolor, A., W. L. Scarpetti, and P. A. Lane, 1967. Teachers' attitudes toward children's behavior revisited. *Journal of Educational Psychology,* 58, 3, 175–180.

U.S. Department of Health, Education, and Welfare, 1958. *Educating Children in Grades Four, Five and Six,* Bulletin No. 3. Washington, D.C.: Government Printing Office.

U.S. Office of Economic Opportunity, 1972. *An Experiment in Performance Contracting: Summary of Preliminary Results.* OEO Pamphlet 3400-5.

Ward, A. W., 1963. *Efficiency and Effectiveness of Group Testing to Pre-screen Children for Exceptional Children Services.* Paper presented at AERA Annual Meeting, Chicago, February 15, 1963.

Weber, L., 1971. *The English Infant School and Informal Education.* Englewood Cliffs, N.J. Prentice-Hall.

Weiner, M. and W. Murray, 1963. Another look at the culturally deprived and their levels of aspiration. *Journal of Educational Sociology,* 36, 319–321.

Wesman, A. G., 1968. Intelligent testing. *American Psychologist,* 23, 4, 267–274.

Westman, J. C., D. L. Rice, and E. Bermann, 1967. Nursery school behavior and later school adjustment. *American Journal of Orthopsychiatry,* 37, 725–731.

Wickman, E. K., 1928. *Children's Behavior and Teachers' Attitudes.* New York: Commonwealth Fund.

Woodring, P., 1970. *Investment in Innovation.* Boston: Little, Brown and Co.

Wrightstone, J. W., 1957. *Class Organization for Instruction.* Washington, D.C.: National Education Association.

# APPENDIX

**Table 1  Coefficients of Correlation between Citywide Standardized Tests Grades 1 through 9—Jefferson School, Total Basic Population**

| | Reading Readiness | Pintner-Cunningham | Otis Alpha | Grade 3 Reading | Otis Beta | Grade 6 Reading | Grade 6 Math | Grade 9 Reading | Pintner Intermediate |
|---|---|---|---|---|---|---|---|---|---|
| Reading Readiness | | | | | | | | | |
| Pintner-Cunningham | .57 | | | | | | | | |
| Otis Alpha | .40 | .60 | | | | | | | |
| Grade 3 Reading | .58 | .56 | .52 | | | | | | |
| Otis Beta | .62 | .58 | .56 | .78 | | | | | |
| Grade 6 Reading | .56 | .45 | .42 | .80 | .84 | | | | |
| Grade 6 Math | .44 | .54 | .58 | .69 | .72 | .73 | | | |
| Grade 9 Reading | .56 | .44 | .41 | .75 | .77 | .81 | .68 | | |
| Pintner Intermediate | .49 | .54 | .50 | .76 | .82 | .79 | .78 | .75 | |

**Chronology of Testing Program**

Grade 1  The New York Reading Readiness Test
Pintner-Cunningham Primary Test

Grade 3  Otis Quick-Scoring Mental Ability Tests—Alpha
Metropolitan Achievement Tests—Reading (appropriate level)

Grade 6  Otis Quick-Scoring Mental Ability Tests—Beta
Metropolitan Achievement Tests—Reading
Metropolitan Achievement Tests—Mathematics—Intermediate

Grade 9  Metropolitan Achievement Tests—Reading
Pintner General Ability Test—Intermediate

**Table 2  Coefficients of Correlation between Citywide Standardized Tests Grades 1 through 9—Jefferson School**

BOYS (upper right) / GIRLS (lower left)

| | Reading Readiness | Pintner-Cunningham | Otis Alpha | Grade 3 Reading | Otis Beta | Grade 6 Reading | Grade 6 Math | Grade 9 Reading | Pintner Intermediate |
|---|---|---|---|---|---|---|---|---|---|
| Reading Readiness | | .58 | .35 | .55 | .56 | .47 | .32 | .45 | .45 |
| Pintner-Cunningham | .56 | | .65 | .58 | .52 | .36 | .46 | .45 | .51 |
| Otis Alpha | .46 | .56 | | .54 | .56 | .44 | .46 | .43 | .44 |
| Grade 3 Reading | .65 | .56 | .50 | | .80 | .79 | .68 | .73 | .81 |
| Otis Beta | .69 | .69 | .59 | .80 | | .85 | .68 | .81 | .82 |
| Grade 6 Reading | .66 | .59 | .43 | .86 | .81 | | .72 | .84 | .79 |
| Grade 6 Math | .55 | .65 | .74 | .78 | .79 | .75 | | .70 | .73 |
| Grade 9 Reading | .63 | .43 | .41 | .81 | .72 | .77 | .65 | | .78 |
| Pintner Intermediate | .53 | .58 | .63 | .74 | .81 | .77 | .81 | .71 | |

Table 3  Coefficients of Correlation between Citywide Standardized Tests
Grades 1 through 9—Washington School, Total Basic Population

| | Reading Readiness | Pintner-Cunning-ham | Otis Alpha | Grade 3 Reading | Otis Beta | Grade 6 Reading | Grade 6 Math | Grade 9 Reading | Pintner Inter-mediate |
|---|---|---|---|---|---|---|---|---|---|
| Reading Readiness | | | | | | | | | |
| Pintner-Cunningham | .53 | | | | | | | | |
| Otis Alpha | .46 | .63 | | | | | | | |
| Grade 3 Reading | .55 | .43 | .59 | | | | | | |
| Otis Beta | .49 | .55 | .63 | .76 | | | | | |
| Grade 6 Reading | .49 | .45 | .61 | .80 | .83 | | | | |
| Grade 6 Math | .44 | .52 | .62 | .78 | .73 | .80 | | | |
| Grade 9 Reading | .47 | .54 | .56 | .74 | .77 | .84 | .72 | | |
| Pintner Intermediate | .40 | .55 | .53 | .70 | .82 | .83 | .82 | .76 | |

Table 4  Coefficients of Correlation between Citywide Standardized Tests Grades 1 through 9—Washington School

| | Reading Readiness | Pintner-Cunningham | Otis Alpha | Grade 3 Reading | Otis Beta | Grade 6 Reading | Grade 6 Math | Grade 9 Reading | Pintner Intermediate | |
|---|---|---|---|---|---|---|---|---|---|---|
| | | | | | | | | BOYS | | |
| Reading Readiness | | .57 | .47 | .61 | .52 | .50 | .55 | .57 | .53 | Reading Readiness |
| Pintner-Cunningham | .52 | | .50 | .25 | .41 | .28 | .30 | .57 | .53 | Pintner-Cunningham |
| Otis Alpha | .47 | .74 | | .66 | .70 | .66 | .66 | .64 | .63 | Otis Alpha |
| Grade 3 Reading | .50 | .65 | .58 | | .76 | .81 | .78 | .73 | .69 | Grade 3 Reading |
| Otis Beta | .46 | .70 | .59 | .76 | | .89 | .80 | .82 | .89 | Otis Beta |
| Grade 6 Reading | .48 | .63 | .60 | .80 | .77 | | .83 | .79 | .87 | Grade 6 Reading |
| Grade 6 Math | .36 | .69 | .63 | .79 | .70 | .80 | | .71 | .89 | Grade 6 Math |
| Grade 9 Reading | .38 | .54 | .52 | .76 | .73 | .88 | .73 | | .78 | Grade 9 Reading |
| Pintner Intermediate | .26 | .64 | .43 | .75 | .78 | .80 | .82 | .75 | | Pintner Intermediate |
| | | | | GIRLS | | | | | | |

163

THE LONGITUDINAL STUDY

Form for Children Showing Difficulty
in Separating from Mother*

Class_____Year_____Name_____Boy__Girl__

Date of          Age at          Nursery School
Entrance_____Entrance_____ Experience:    Yes__No__

Kg. Orientation: Yes__No__    Parent Interview: Yes__No__

Was there any indication from interview that there
would be any difficulty?

| TIME AT SCHOOL | SIGNS OF DIFFICULTY | TIME MOTHER HAD TO STAY AND REACTION |
|---|---|---|
| First Day | | |
| First Week | | |
| Second Week | | |
| Later until acute symptoms ended | | |

What handling seemed to help?

What handling had no effect or aggravated
the difficulty?

_____
*Original form provided adequate space for answers.

164

| CHILD'S REACTION TO: | FIRST TWO WEEKS | ANY CHANGES AT END OF ACUTE PERIOD | AT END OF SIX MONTHS |
|---|---|---|---|
| Children | | | |
| Teacher | | | |
| Materials | | | |
| New Experiences or Change in Routines | | | |
| Parent | | | |

Additional Comments:

*Original form provided adequate space for answers.

THE LONGITUDINAL STUDY

Teacher's Estimate of Reading Development

| Name of Child | Competence in Reading | | | | Interest in Reading | | | | Comments |
|---|---|---|---|---|---|---|---|---|---|
| | Not Ready for Reading | Just Beginning to Read | Reading What Level? | Marked | Average | Very Little | Aversion | | |
| | | | | | | | | | |
| | | | | | | | | | |
| | | | | | | | | | |
| | | | | | | | | | |
| | | | | | | | | | |
| | | | | | | | | | |
| | | | | | | | | | |
| | | | | | | | | | |
| | | | | | | | | | |

School_____Class_____Teacher_____Date_____

## Teacher's Estimate of Intelligence

| Name of Child | Exceptional | Bright | Average | Dull | Possibly Retarded | Comments |
|---|---|---|---|---|---|---|
|  |  |  |  |  |  |  |
|  |  |  |  |  |  |  |
|  |  |  |  |  |  |  |
|  |  |  |  |  |  |  |
|  |  |  |  |  |  |  |
|  |  |  |  |  |  |  |
|  |  |  |  |  |  |  |
|  |  |  |  |  |  |  |
|  |  |  |  |  |  |  |
|  |  |  |  |  |  |  |
|  |  |  |  |  |  |  |
|  |  |  |  |  |  |  |

School_____Class_____Teacher_____Date_____

167

## Attitude Toward Classroom Activity

Rate each child by checking the column that indicates his usual reaction to classroom activities. Please comment on situations or activities that engender a reaction other than the one checked, or in any case where your comments would help to give a more complete picture of the child's attitude and reactions. List boys and girls on separate sheets.

| Name of Child | Enthusiastic | Interested | Passive | Uninterested | Resistant | Comments |
|---|---|---|---|---|---|---|
| | | | | | | |
| | | | | | | |
| | | | | | | |
| | | | | | | |
| | | | | | | |
| | | | | | | |
| | | | | | | |

School_____ Class_____ Teacher_____ Date_____

THE LONGITUDINAL STUDY

## General Adjustment Rating Scale

Rate each child according to your estimate of the child's
general adjustment by checking in the appropriate column
of this five-point scale.  Rating 1 indicates very good
adjustment; rating 5 indicates very poor adjustment;
rating 2, 3, 4 indicate variations between 1 and 5.  If
you think that a child needs specialized help beyond
that which can be given by the classroom teacher, place
a check under "Needs"; if the child is already receiving
assistance from some source or agency outside of your
classroom, name such source or agency under "Receiving."
List boys and girls on separate sheets.

| Name of Child | RATING SCALE | | | | | SPECIALIZED HELP | | COMMENTS Problems,etc. |
|---|---|---|---|---|---|---|---|---|
| | 1 | 2 | 3 | 4 | 5 | Needs | Receiving | |
| | | | | | | | | |
| | | | | | | | | |
| | | | | | | | | |
| | | | | | | | | |
| | | | | | | | | |
| | | | | | | | | |
| | | | | | | | | |
| | | | | | | | | |

School_____Class_____Teacher_____Date_____

169

## Adjustment Problems

| Name<br>of<br>Child | Problem<br>(describe briefly) | Comments |
|---|---|---|
| | | |

School_____Class_____Reg._____Teacher_____Date_____

THE LONGITUDINAL STUDY

## Gifted Children

| Name of Child | Giftedness (describe) | Comments |
|---|---|---|
|  |  |  |

School_____Class_____Reg._____Teacher_____Date_____

## THE LONGITUDINAL STUDY

## Parent Questionnaire*

### (Grade 1)

Child's Name_____Class_____School_____

Does your child usually like to go          Yes__No__
to school?

Is there anything he especially likes        Yes__No__
at school?

Is there anything about school that          Yes__No__
worries him?
        If so, what?

How has going to school helped your child?

Is there any special help you would like     Yes__No__
the school to give him?
        If so, what help?

Has your child any health or physical        Yes__No__
problems the school should know about in
order to help him?
        If so, please explain.

Has your child ever had a serious accident?  Yes__No__
        If he has, what happened?    When?

_____
*Original form provided adequate space for answers.

172

Has your child ever been hospitalized?        Yes__No__
      If he has, for how long and for
      <u>what reason</u>?     <u>When</u>?

What special interests does he show
outside of school?

Does he enjoy playing with other children?   Yes__No__
      With younger children?         Yes__No__
      With older children?           Yes__No__
      With children his own age?    Yes__No__

How does he get along at home?

Would you like to meet with               Yes__No__
Mrs._____, the Project
Assistant, to discuss any
of these matters?

Father's occupation_____

Mother's Occupation_____

Signature_____

If you wish to write any additional comments, please
do so on the other side of this paper.

THE LONGITUDINAL STUDY

Parent Questionnaire*

(Grade 3)

As you probably know, your child is in a group that is part of a special study being conducted by the Board of Education. By observing children over a period of years we hope to gain information which will be of great value, not only in helping your child, but in helping children throughout the city.

To carry out this task, we need your assistance. Please be good enough to answer the questions below, giving as much information as you can. Use the other side of the page if you need more space. Your answers will be kept confidential. If you come to a question which you do not wish to answer, omit it and go on to the next. Please be sure to answer these questions in full and return this questionnaire in the envelope provided. We very much appreciate your cooperation.

Child's Name_____ Class_____School_____

Does your child usually like school?          Yes___ No___
    Comments:

Is there anything he (she) especially          Yes___ No___
likes at school?
    If so, please tell what.

Is there anything about school that            Yes___ No___
worries him (her)?
    If so, please tell what.

_____
*Original form provided adequate space for answers.

174

Is there any special help you would like          Yes___No___
the school to give him (her)?
    If so, what help?


Are you satisfied with your child's               Yes___No___
work in school?
    Please explain.


Is your child satisfied with his (her)            Yes___No___
work in school?
    Please explain.


What special interests does he (she)
show outside of school?


Does he (she) present any problems at home? Yes___No___
    Comments:


What qualities would you like him (her)
to develop further?


Has your child any health or physical             Yes___No___
problems at present, that the school
should know about?
    If so, please explain.


Has your child had a serious accident             Yes___No___
within the past two years?
    If he (she) has, what happened?  When?

Has your child been hospitalized within        Yes__No__
the past two years?
      If he (she) has, for how long
      and for what reason?      When?


Would you like to meet with                     Yes__No__
Mrs._____, the Project
Assistant to discuss any of these matters?


Additional Comments:

THE LONGITUDINAL STUDY

## Parent Questionnaire*

(Grade 6)


As you probably know, your child is in a group that is part of a special study being conducted by the Board of Education. By observing children over a period of years we hope to gain information which will be of great value, not only in helping your child, but in helping children throughout the city.

To carry out this task, we need your assistance. Please be good enough to answer the questions below, giving as much information as you can. Use the other side of the page if you need more space. Your answers will be kept confidential. Please return this questionnaire in the envelope provided. We very much appreciate your cooperation.


Child's Name_____ Class_____School_____


Does your child usually like school?


Is there anything your child especially likes at school? If so, what?


Is there anything about school that worries your child? If so, what?


Are you satisfied with the progress your child has made in the elementary school?
    Comments:

_____
*Original form provided adequate space for answers.

Do you think your child is satisfied with the progress
he (she) has made in the elementary school?
    Comments:


What special interests does your child show outside of
school?


What do you think are your child's strong points?


What do you think are your child's weak points?


Does your child have any special talents?
    If so, what?


What qualities would you like your child to develop
further?


Does your child present any problems at home?
    If so, what?


In the elementary school do you think your child has
learned:

      more than you expected? _____

      as much as you expected?_____

      less than you expected? _____


How does your child feel about going to junior
high school?

Is there any special help that you would like the
junior high school to give your child?
    If so, what?


Do you expect your child to go to high school?_____
to college?_____


What would you like your child to do for a living when
he (she) grows up?


Has your child any health or physical problems at
present?
    If so, please explain.


Has your child ever been hospitalized?

    When?            How long?        For what reason?


Has your child ever had a serious accident, injury
or illness?

    What?                            When?


If there is anything else you would like to tell us
about your child, please do so.


Father's occupation_____

Mother's occupation_____

Signature_____

## Parent Questionnaire*

(Grade 9)

As you probably know, your child has been in a group that has been studied since his or her early days in elementary school.  By observing children over a period of years we hope to gain information which will be of great value, not only in helping your child, but in helping children throughout the city.

To carry out this task, we need your assistance. Please be good enough to answer the questions below, giving as much information as you can.  Use the other side of the page if you need more space.  Your answers will be kept confidential.  Please return this question- naire in the envelope provided.  We very much appreciate your cooperation.


Child's Name_____ Class_____ School_____


Does your child usually like school?


Is there anything your child especially likes at school?
     If so, what?


Is there anything about school that worries your child?
     If so, what?


Are you satisfied with the progress your child has made in the junior high school?
     Comments:

_____
*Original form provided adequate space for answers.

Do you think your child is satisfied with the progress
he (she) has made in the junior high school?
    Comments:


In the junior high school do you think your child
has learned:

    more than you expected? _____

    as much as you expected?_____

    less than you expected? _____


Is there any special help that you would like the
high school to give your child?
    If so, what?


Do you expect your child to go to college?_____


What would you like your child to do for a living when
he (she) grows up?


Over the years that your child has attended school, have
there been any important changes in attitudes toward
school, in habits of work, in behavior?

If there is anything else you would like to tell us about your child, please do so.


Father's occupation_____

Mother's occupation_____

Signature_____

THE LONGITUDINAL STUDY

## Children's Questionnaire*

(Grades 2 and 5)

NAME_____     BOY_____ GIRL_____

SCHOOL_____ CLASS_____     DATE_____

1. What was the most fun you ever had?

2. If you could have one wish what would it be?

3. What do you like best in school?

4. What do you like best outside of school?

5. What don't you like in school?

6. What don't you like outside of school?

7. What do you wish you were?

8. When are you happy?

9. When do you get mad?

_____
*Original form provided adequate space for answers.

10. What makes you afraid?

11. Remember when you first started school?  How did you feel?

12. What do you remember about when you were in kindergarten?

13. What do you remember about when you were in first grade?

14. What do you like best about yourself?

15. What do the children in your class like best about you?

16. What do you want to be when you grow up?

THE LONGITUDINAL STUDY

## Children's Questionnaire*

(Grade 6)

NAME_____    BOY_____GIRL_____

SCHOOL_____ CLASS_____    DATE_____

1. What I liked best about my elementary school days was

2. When I'm not in school I like to

3. When I'm not in school I don't like to

4. If I could be anyone, I would like to be

5. I am happy when

6. I get mad when

7. I'm afraid when

8. I worry about

9. When I first started school I felt

_____
*Original form provided adequate space for answers.

10. What I did not like about elementary school was

11. What I like about myself is

12. What my classmates like best about me is

13. The way I feel about school is

14. What I do best is

15. Going to junior high school makes me feel

16. When I get to junior high school I would like special help in

17. The things about myself I would like to improve are

18. Are you satisfied with how you made out in the elementary school?

19. Do you expect to go to high school?

20. Do you expect to go to college?

21. What do you want to be when you grow up?

# THE LONGITUDINAL STUDY

## Children's Questionnaire*

(Grade 9)

NAME_____     BOY_____ GIRL_____

SCHOOL_____ CLASS_____     DATE_____

1. What did you like best about elementary school?

2. Remember when you first started school?  How did you feel?

3. What did you like least about elementary school?

4. What subjects, if any, do you find hard?

5. What do you like best about junior high school?

6. What do you like least about junior high school?

7. What do you remember, if anything, about kindergarten or first grade?

8. What do you like to do after school?

_____

*Original form provided adequate space for answers.

9.  What do you think are your strong points?

10. What are your weaknesses?

11. If you could be anyone, like whom would you most prefer to be?

12. What do you worry about?

13. What do you think you do best?

14. What do you want to be when you grow up?

15. Are you satisfied with your achievement (progress) in junior high school?

16. What do your parents think of your achievement in junior high school?

17. If you could get special help in school, what kind, if any, do you think you need?

18. If you had your choice of any high school in the city, what high school would you like to attend?

19. Do you expect to go to college?

THE LONGITUDINAL STUDY


## Student Questionnaire*

### High School Information

1.  What did you like best about high school?


2.  What subjects did you have trouble with?


3.  What subjects were easiest for you?


4.  What subjects did you find most interesting?


5.  Did you develop any new interests while in
    high school?
        If so, what are they?


6.  Did you take part in any school organization, club,
    or team?
        If so, which?


7.  Did you win any honors or awards, e.g., Arista, etc.?
        If so, which?


8.  What problems did you have during your high
    school years?


9.  Are you satisfied with your achievement in
    high school?
        Please explain.

---

*Given upon graduation from high school. Original
 form provided adequate space for answers.

10. Are your parents satisfied with your achievement in high school?

11. If you could start over again, which high school would you choose?
    What course or diploma?

12. What course have you now completed?

## Vocational Plans

1. What are your plans after graduation?

2. Do you think your school has prepared you adequately for this?

3. Did you apply for college?  If yes, list the colleges to which you applied in order of your preference.

4. Place a check after each one that accepted you.

5. To which college are you going?

6. What would you really like to do for a living?

7.  What would your parents like you to do?


8.  What do you think you'll be doing five years
    from now?


## General Information

1.  What do you think are your strong points?


2.  What are your weaknesses?


3.  What do you think you do best?


4.  You may remember that we know you since you
    started school.  Can you describe how you felt and
    what happened on that first day?


5.  In which school do you think you made the greatest
    progress?  Elementary_____Junior High School_____
    High School_____


6.  In which of these schools did you have the best
    teachers?  Elementary_____Junior High School_____
    High School_____


7.  Can you describe the characteristics of the best
    teacher you have had?

**DATE DUE**

| | | | |
|---|---|---|---|
| | | | |
| | | | |
| | | | |
| | | | |
| | | | |
| | | | |
| | | | |
| | | | |
| | | | |
| | | | |
| | | | |
| | | | |
| | | | |
| | | | |
| | | | |
| | | | |
| | | | |
| | | | |
| GAYLORD | | | PRINTED IN U.S.A. |